The Latest
Air Fryer
Cookbook UK

Easy & Amazing Air Fryer Recipes to Help You Create Gourmet Meals
for Family and Friends (Suitable for Beginners and Advanced Users)

Annabelle Bostic

Table of Contents

Chapter 3 Fish and Seafood Recipes 38

Chapter 4 Poultry Recipes 50

Chapter 5 Beef, Pork, and Lamb Recipes

Chapter 6 Snack and Starter Recipes....78

Nearly all kitchens are tight on counter space. Even when you have a lot of it, it's simple to fill with the newest kitchen gadgets and get cluttered. You should, however, create place for an air fryer.

An air fryer is similar to an oven in that it bakes and roasts food, but it differs from an oven in that it uses less oil than a conventional oven and has heating elements that are only on the top. This makes food incredibly crispy in a matter of minutes. Due of the focused heat source and the positioning and size of the fan, air fryers typically heat up very quickly and cook food quickly and evenly.

The clean-up is just another fantastic benefit of air frying. Most baskets and racks for air fryers can go in the dishwasher. We advise using a decent dish brush, such as this one from Casabella, for any dishes that cannot be put in the dishwasher. Without making you crazy, it will reach every nook and cranny that helps with air circulation.

A countertop gadget called an air fryer essentially functions as a small convection oven. It uses heat and airflow from an internal fan instead of a lot of oil or fat to crisp up the chips and cook your chicken wings evenly.

What is Air Fryer?

The air fryer is an ubiquitous kitchen appliance for frying foods like meat, pastries, and potato chips.

Heated air is blown around the dish to produce a crunchy, crispy surface.

This also leads to the Maillard reaction, a chemical process. When heat is present, the reaction between an amino acid and a reducing sugar alters the colour and flavour of food

Air-fried foods are marketed as a healthier alternative to deep-fried ones due to their lower fat and calorie content.

Food can be air-fried with just a tablespoon (15 mL) of oil and still come out tasting and feeling like it was deep-fried.

Benefits of Using It

Healthy

An air fryer uses significantly less oil than a deep fryer, which is its principal health advantage. A large portion of the utilized oil also drains away without being absorbed by the food. As a result, you consume fewer calories and fat.

These fryers' convection method encourages the Maillard reaction, a chemical process that results in browning. This has the added benefit of making the food look better while also enhancing its flavour while having less fat.

Crispier Cuisine

Being able to generate crispy food without using oil is one of the best features of air fryers. They accomplish this by enclosing food in a perforated basket or on a rack with extremely hot air from all sides utilizing convection-style heating.

As a result, air fryers are ideal for producing crispy chips, onion rings, fish fingers, and other conventional fried food kinds.

Because it can cover the entire surface of the meal and because the frying basket allows any excess fat to drop away, an air fryer yields crispier results than a conventional convection oven.

Quicker

Air fryers cook food far more quickly than the majority of traditional alternative ways because of how they operate. The rapid frying procedure is made possible by maintaining and constantly circulating the tremendous heat generated inside the fryer.

Many versions either don't need to be heated up before use or only take a little time to do so. Depending on the particular meals, cooking times can be cut by more than 30 to 50 percent as compared to using a standard oven.

Fewer Messes

Compared to deep fryers, air fryers are much less dirty. That's because the cooking procedure only requires a small amount of oil, and it's this that makes the bulk of the mess.

An air fryer may be cleaned most easily with a soft-bristle brush, dish soap, and water.

Secure

Air fryers are generally safer because they are self-contained appliances and because little hot fat is used in the cooking process. Splashes and burns are less of a problem.

In order to prevent the food from burning, machines are also made to turn off when the timer expires.

More Adaptable
An air fryer can be used to prepare most dishes that are typically cooked in a deep fryer just as well or even better. There are numerous recipes to experiment with. Surprisingly, baked items, vegetables, and steaks all perform nicely.

Avoid Distributing Heat and Odor
Air fryers retain heat, so unlike conventional ovens, they don't raise the temperature of your kitchen. If you reside in a smaller home or apartment, this quality is especially helpful.
Due to the small amount of oil needed, there aren't any of the intense aromas that can come from deep frying.

Smaller in Size
Kitchen equipment like air fryers are comparatively small; they are a little larger than toasters. They work well in spaces where size can be an issue, like a small kitchen.
They may be utilized in an RV or camper while traveling, as well as on a campsite, thanks to their ease of portability.

Reasonable
Air fryers are surprisingly affordable to purchase, especially given how practical and adaptable they are. They normally cost between $50 and $150 and are offered by online sellers.

However, I would advise avoiding the less expensive models and choosing quality even if it costs a bit more.

Simple to Use
Most of the time, air fryers are quite simple to use and require little supervision during cooking. Simply place the food into the basket, set the timer and temperature, and let the fryer handle the rest.
If you need any inspiration, there are several simple recipes available. I find frying veggies to be really simple and gratifying; the roasting effect makes the vegetables appetizing.

Great for Vegetable
Are you and the people you love finicky eaters of vegetables? Vegetables can be crisped up and made tastier by air frying. Many individuals find that air-frying vegetables like cauliflower, broccoli, or Brussels sprouts improves their texture. There are also a tonne of recipes available online that offer choices for breading veggies to cook in an air fryer (like the buffalo cauliflower below). Some even include healthier alternatives like crumbs made from grains or chickpeas. This is especially useful if you're aiming to increase the number of plant-based meals in your weekly menu or follow a plant-based diet.

Step-By-Step Air Frying

Setup before First Use

You should take off all of the stickers and the air fryer's packing before using it for the first time. After that, place on a solid, heat-resistant surface.

Make sure the air fryer is set up far from surfaces and items. This will stop steam from doing any harm.

You should remove the basket from the air fryer using the handle in order to get rid of all the plastic packaging. Utilize the basket release button to separate the inner and outer baskets.

Use a non-abrasive sponge or a dishwasher to thoroughly clean both baskets. With a slightly moist towel, clean the basket's interior and outside.

The basket can be dried with a dry towel. Put the basket back inside the air fryer after that.

The Air Fryer Is Running a Test

Before utilising the air fryer for cooking, you should test it at least once.

This will assist you in becoming familiar with the various features of your air fryer and ensuring that it is operating properly.

The air fryer can be examined as follows: Connect the air fryer's power plug. A full air fryer basket should be used. Next, give the air fryer some time to warm up.

You will see a preheat button on your air fryer if it has multiple functions. Small, pricey air fryers typically use analogue control systems.

These will need to be manually warmed up. In order to manually preheat, heat for 5 minutes at 400°F. When the preheating process is finished, the air fryer will beep. After that, remove the air fryer's basket and give it five minutes to cool. After that, re-place the empty basket inside the air fryer.

Decide on the time and temperature you want. Now check to see if the air fryer is operating correctly. The air fryer will automatically switch off and keep making the "beep beep" sound when the cooking time is up.

Then, using the handle, remove the air fryer basket, allowing it to cool for 10 to 30 minutes. If everything goes as planned, your air fryer will be prepared for use.

A Few Pointers for the Air Fryer Basket Only remove the air fryer's basket when cooking and cleaning food. Avoid repeatedly removing the basket. The handle's button guard stops the user from unintentionally hitting the release button. To release the basket, slide the button guard forward. When taking out the basket, never hit the basket release button. This is because the basket may fall and create mishaps if the release button is pressed while the basket is being carried. When you're ready, merely press the basket release button. Make sure the surface you plan to set it on is secure and heat-resistant. The air fryer's handle is affixed to the inside basket rather than the outside basket. As a result, your outer basket will drop when you press the release button on the basket.

A Few Pointers for the Air Fryer Basket Only remove the air fryer's basket when cooking and cleaning food.

Avoid repeatedly removing the basket. The handle's button guard stops the user from unintentionally hitting the release button.

To release the basket, slide the button guard forward. When taking out the basket, never hit the basket release button.

This is because the basket may fall and create mishaps if the release button is pressed while the basket is being carried.

When you're ready, merely press the basket release button. Make sure the surface you plan to set it on is secure and heat-resistant.

The air fryer's handle is affixed to the inside basket rather than the outside basket. As a result, your outer basket will drop when you press the release button on the basket.

An Instruction Guide

It is necessary to heat up the air fryer before using it to cook. This is done so that once the air fryer is preheated, the food would cook more quickly and have a crispy exterior.

A multi-purpose device can be instantly pre-heated by pressing the preheat button. However, manual preheating is required for little, low-cost air fryers.

The air fryer needs to be manually preheated for five minutes at 400°F. After the air fryer has finished preheating, remove the air fryer basket and add the food.

However, keep in mind that the basket shouldn't include too much food. because if the basket is overfilled, the food may not be cooked properly. After filling the air fryer basket with food, place it inside the appliance.

Next, decide when and at what temperature meals should be served. While cooking, you can also change the temperature and time.

Start the air fryer by pressing the start button.. But after you start cooking, you have to keep an eye on it to make sure it doesn't get too done or burnt.

You can combine the ingredients midway through cooking or flip the meal over to ensure that it is thoroughly cooked.

When the cooking time is up, the air fryer will beep. Next, take out the air fryer basket. But mind the heat of the steam.

After separating the inner and outer baskets, serve the food. Separate the inner from the outer basket while keeping the basket on a flat surface. The basket must completely cool before cleaning.

What Is an Air Fryer's Mechanism?

Let's first talk about an air fryer's operation before moving on to its uses and advantages.

In order to provide the same level of crispiness as traditional fried dishes, air fryers work by moving hot air around a food product. By eliminating high-fat and high-calorie oils from the cooking process, these have the desired impact. Compared to other deep-frying methods, the air fryer uses a very small amount of oil. Instead of using many cups of oil, you may cook your favourite foods using just one scoop.

Around the food, heated air that can reach 400 degrees Fahrenheit is pushed by a fan. Similar to deep-fried dishes, the foods are cooked on the outside first by the circulating air, leaving the interiors mushy. The bottom of the dish has a basket where any grease, if any, is collected from the food.

According to research, air fryers employ heated air with tiny oil droplets to remove moisture from the meal. As a result, it yields fried meals of the same type but with substantially less fat.

The Millard effect, which air fryers cause to happen, enhances the colour and flavour of the food they fry. So, the main question here is, "What does an air fryer do?"

Important Things to Keep in Mind

• Constantly keep the grate in the basket. This allows hot air to circulate around the food and keeps it from resting in additional oil.

• Air fryers emit a sound. You can hear the fans rotating when it's running.

• It is useful. To ensure equal browning, remove the basket every few minutes and turn the food around. You are welcome to remove the basket and examine it. Any time during the cooking process is OK for doing this. There is no need to turn off the machine because it shuts off when the basket is removed.

• Check if the drawer is fully inserted as a result to avoid a fault. The air fryer will alert you by suddenly going silent.

• You're not used to how rapidly food cooks! It's one of the nicest aspects about the air fryer. In the manual for your air fryer, there is probably a helpful table with frying times and temperatures for common foods.

• If there is less food in the basket, the cook time will be cut; if there is more food, the cook time will be extended. You might need a slightly lower temperature. Many air fryer recipes call for lower temperature settings than traditional recipes. Even if this might seem dubious, believe it.

• A slightly lower temperature will help prevent food from being excessively black or crispy on the exterior while still ensuring that the inside is cooked through because air fryers heat up rapidly and circulate the hot air.

Straight from Store

Size and Volume

Size is an important factor, particularly if your kitchen is small. A medium-sized air fryer can hold between 3.7 and 4.1 litres of food. They are so little that they should easily fit in most kitchens. However, there is a clear correlation between size and capacity. Choosing a small or medium-sized fryer may compel you to cook meals in batches, which you don't want to do if you have a large family or frequently host parties.

Make your pick carefully because larger air fryers tend to be bulkier and can cook food more quickly for more people.

Controls

Most air fryers have dials for managing the temperature and timer. If you want more accuracy, look for higher-end models with digital controls. Even the ability to establish custom temperatures and LED displays that display information are included. Additionally, these air fryers include settings that make frying simpler. Additionally, keep an eye out for the rapidly expanding category of intelligent air fryers. They have Wi-Fi connectivity, allowing you to control cooking settings from your phone.

Cleaning

Regularly cleaning your air fryer completely is essential. Thankfully, cleaning an air fryer doesn't require a lot of work. Simply take out its drawer and wash it while turning on the water. The inside basket, which is frequently removable, can be fully washed with dishwashing detergent. These baskets' non-stick coating often prevents food from sticking. Some variants also feature a dishwasher-safe construction.

Air fryers allow for the rapid and simple preparation of healthy cuisine without sacrificing flavour. The majority of chefs suggest reducing cooking or baking times by 20% because this expedites food preparation. For instance, air frying for 24 minutes should be sufficient if the original recipe asks for conventional cooking for 30 minutes. Users must also experiment with temperature settings to avoid overcooking. You can use free tools like the Oven to Air Fryer converter to calculate the correct temperature and cooking time for oven recipes. Chefs frequently advise spraying or brushing some oil on the food halfway through cooking to increase browning and crispiness.

Cleaning and Caring for Your Air Fryer

There are several different types of air fryers available. None, of course, are as stylish or well-made as Ree's! For comprehensive instructions, it is therefore advisable to periodically review the owner's manual for your particular model. But by giving an air fryer a fast once-over at the very least after every other usage, cleaning one is made simple. Chelsea suggests cleaning anything you make that is particularly messy, such as something with sauce or marinade, the same day to prevent a stuck-on mess. Mae Plummer is the author of Mae's Menu's recipes. "It gets tougher to remove anything from the air fryer the longer something sticks."

Cleaning your air fryer on a regular basis will not only make the task simpler, but it will also stop the accumulation of food particles that could otherwise result in issues, unpleasant odours, or even—worst case scenario—a fire. The quickest and simplest method to quickly clean your air fryer is as follows:
Before unplugging your fryer after usage, allow it to cool completely.

The basket, tray, or other item should be removed and washed in the sink with warm water and dish soap. Drying is more effective at night.
Use a moist, soapy cloth, sponge, or paper towel to clean the inside of the fryer, being especially careful to protect the heating element. Use a damp cloth to reclean the area, then dry it off.
Use a gentle towel to clean the fryer's outside.
Place the removable frying parts inside the fryer once they have dried.
How should I thoroughly clean my air fryer?
The process is largely the same as the quick cleanup you do after cooking, with a few more stages. According to chef Sylvia Fountaine, air fryers are really just little convection ovens with a nonstick drawer. Feasting at Home is her recipe blog. You can therefore treat caked-on food similarly to how you would treat a non-stick pan. "The air fryer basket needs to have a cup of water filled. After a brief period of intense heat, the air fryer should be turned off. Debris and cooked-on fat are easily removed using heat and water. Opening the drawer reveals that a significant amount of dirt was rapidly eliminated without the use of soap or washing."

Are your fryer's removable parts still filthy? Use a toothbrush with soft bristles to gently scrub them after 30 minutes in hot, soapy water. A toothpick can be used to (gently) reach places that are challenging to clean, including the perforations in the grate. Never, however, should the entire air fryer be filled with water.

How Can Sticky Residue Be Removed from an Air Fryer?
Try Fountaine's procedure, but if the inside of your air fryer feels unusually oily, add a little dish soap to the water. Use a grease-fighting product like Dawn Ultra if at all possible. To make cleaning the air fryer after use simpler, you might also be able to use disposable aluminium foil or parchment paper liners. Please make sure they are compatible with your toaster oven air fryer by reading your owner's handbook.

Clean Up the Sham Right Away
Get into the habit of wiping out grease and food residue as soon as you can because doing so will make it more difficult to remove them later. This is especially true if you leave them in the air fryer overnight or for several days at a time. After every usage, give your air fryer a good cleaning even if you don't immediately get around to a deeper clean. This will stop the oils from drying out. Additionally, clean up any crumbs left over after using the air fryer. Another straightforward option is to immediately wash the air fryer basket after use with warm, soapy water, then clean it later when it's more convenient.

Prepare Your Basket
By lining your frying basket, you can significantly reduce the amount of cleanup required after cooking. Find a dishwasher-safe, easily removable basket insert if you can. You won't have to deep clean your air fryer as regularly as a result. If you can't find one, you may just use parchment paper or tin foil sparingly. To inhibit ventilation and prevent the food from overcooking, do not, however, block the openings in the basket. Additionally, never put tin foil or parchment paper in the bottom of the drawer when using an air fryer.

Be Wary of Non-stick

Customers have complained about the non-stick coating on some air fryer parts wearing off over time on our website and in other places. In spite of the fact that we haven't observed this (our testing evaluates performance immediately out of the box), our advise for other nonstick cookware is still applicable here: If the non-stick coating is peeled, avoid using the air fryer and avoid using steel wool, metal utensils, or any other abrasives as they may scratch or chip the non-stick coating. Instead, attempt phoning the manufacturer's customer care and requesting a new basket, or consider returning the air fryer to the retailer.

Frequently Asked Questions & Notes

Describe the Air Fryer

Large countertop equipment called "air fryers" make a bold claim: wonderfully fried meals using very little oil (often less than a tablespoon). However, an air fryer is not at all a fryer, despite the catchy name. It is a little convection oven that uses a fan to move hot air around food as it cooks. By using convection cooking in this manner, food can be prepared with a similar level of crispiness to fried food but using significantly less oil. However, the extremely hot air is also perfect for roasting and even makes it possible to prepare foods that you would typically grill.

Is Deep Frying Unhealthy?

Yes, the air fryer works as intended: Instead of using quarts of oil, a cook may use a little bit to get perfectly crisp results for chips, poultry, fish, and more. However, we discovered that the outcomes resemble those of an oven-fried dish more so than a deep-fried one. Foods that are air-fried or baked instead of deep-fried taste much thinner because fat is necessary for the "fried" flavour. However, we discovered that food cooked in the greatest air fryers was even better than food cooked in ovens.

Does the Air Fryer Need to Be Preheated?

An oven heats up slower than an air fryer. When creating the recipes for our air fryer cookbook, Air Fryer Perfection, we discovered that the total cooking time for food added to a cold air fryer was the same as when we waited a few minutes for the air fryer to heat up before adding our food. Additionally, skipping the preheating was practical. One benefit of utilising an air fryer rather than an oven is that you can cook food much more quickly because you don't need to pre-heat the appliance.

What Is the Capacity of an Air Fryer?

Depending on the cuisine, most conventional air fryers can fit enough food for 2 to 4 servings. It's crucial to avoid stuffing the basket too full. If you decide to prepare an air frying recipe in multiple batches, begin monitoring the second batch for doneness a few minutes earlier because the air fryer will already The second batch might cook more rapidly if it's hot.

How to Avoid Adhering?

We advise lightly misting the basket with vegetable oil spray before adding dishes that are prone to sticking, like breaded chicken or delicate fish. Additionally, cleanup and the removal of some meals, particularly fish, can be simplified by using a foil sling.

How Can My Air Fryer Be Cleaned?

The majority of the air fryer's removable elements, such the drawer and basket on many versions, are dishwasher-safe, but you should always check the handbook before doing so. Additionally, you should occasionally clean the main body of your air fryer because food splatters and grease can amass around the heating element and result in smoking. Some types' heating elements can be more easily accessed by flipping the air fryer over. Before cleaning the interior of your air fryer, make sure it is fully cool. Use a light detergent. Run the air fryer briefly after cleaning it to help the interior air out.

What should I Do If I Smell Smoke during Air Frying or If the Smell Coming from My Air Fryer Changes?

Keep your air fryer clean! We discovered that a dirty air fryer was the main cause of smoking and odour issues. Make careful to clean the area around the air fryer's heating element to get rid of any accumulated residue if you notice a lot of smoke or smell burning even though your food hasn't really burned. Check periodically for food splatter with a mild detergent while it's cool.

4-Week Diet Plan

Week 1

Day 1:
Breakfast: Savory Potato Hash
Lunch: Delicious Roasted Carrots
Snack: Simple Low-Carb Honey Mustard
Dinner: Juicy Steak Fajitas
Dessert: Perfect Grilled Peaches

Day 2:
Breakfast: Simple Granola
Lunch: Sweet Potato Bites
Snack: Crispy Chicken Wings
Dinner: Chicken Fajitas
Dessert: Simple Blueberry Hand Pies

Day 3:
Breakfast: Simple French Toast Sticks
Lunch: Crispy Roasted Broccoli
Snack: Simple Fried Pickles
Dinner: Delicious Fried Prawn
Dessert: Perfect Beignets

Day 4:
Breakfast: Veggie Cream Frittata
Lunch: Perfect Roasted Broccoli
Snack: Spicy Fried Buffalo Chicken Dip
Dinner: Butter Pork Chops
Dessert: Wonderful Big Chocolate Cookie

Day 5:
Breakfast: Parmesan Veggie Frittata
Lunch: Healthy Kale Chips
Snack: Italian Stuffed Mushroom Caps
Dinner: Breaded Chicken Strips
Dessert: Wonderful Strawberry-Rhubarb Crumble

Day 6:
Breakfast: Milk and Pumpkin Donut Holes
Lunch: Crispy Baby Potatoes
Snack: Air-fryer Egg Rolls
Dinner: Healthy Fried Tilapia
Dessert: Irresistible Churro Bites

Day 7:
Breakfast: Low-Calorie Blueberry Muffins
Lunch: Quick Yeast Rolls
Snack: Bacon Cheeseburger Dip
Dinner: Marinated Steak Kebabs
Dessert: Traditional Apple-Cinnamon Hand Pies

Week 2

Day 1:
Breakfast: Avocado and Egg Burrito
Lunch: Delicious Garlic Bread
Snack: Fried Edamame
Dinner: Chicken Taquitos
Dessert: Delicious Baked Apples

Day 2:
Breakfast: Carrot and Golden Raisin Muffins
Lunch: Zest Fried Aasparagus
Snack: Crunchy Tortilla Chips
Dinner: Amazing Coconut Prawn
Dessert: Unbeatable Gooey Lemon Bars

Day 3:
Breakfast: Crispy Ham Egg Cups
Lunch: Lemon Butter Asparagus
Snack: Italian Toasted Ravioli
Dinner: Breaded Pork Chops
Dessert: Sweet Blueberries Jubilee

Day 4:
Breakfast: Simple Red Pepper and Feta Frittata
Lunch: Versatile Cauliflower Tots
Snack: Spicy Onion Rings
Dinner: Parmesan-crumb Chicken
Dessert: Ultimate Chocolate Bread Pudding

Day 5:
Breakfast: Bagels with Everything
Lunch: Popular Buffalo Cauliflower
Snack: Cheese Pizza Pinwheels
Dinner: Delicious Catfish Bites
Dessert: Delicious Candied Walnuts

Day 6:
Breakfast: Fresh Mixed Berry Muffins
Lunch: Crispy Okra
Snack: Italian Crispy Stuffed Olives
Dinner: Beef Empanadas with Cheeses
Dessert: Delicious Meringue Cookies

Day 7:
Breakfast: Low-Calorie Baked Peach Oatmeal
Lunch: Sweet Brussels Sprouts
Snack: Spinach Artichoke Dip
Dinner: Korean Chicken Wings
Dessert: Luscious "Grilled" Watermelon

Week 3

Day 1:
Breakfast: Jalapeño Egg Cups
Lunch: Classic Green Bean Casserole
Snack: Baked Jalapeño Poppers
Dinner: Great Breaded Calamari
Dessert: Quick and Easy Apple Pie Egg Rolls

Day 2:
Breakfast: Whole Wheat Breakfast Pita
Lunch: Delicious Butternut Squash
Snack: Spicy Fried Chickpeas
Dinner: Barbecued Baby Back Ribs
Dessert: Easy S'more

Day 3:
Breakfast: Chicken Sausages with Black Pepper
Lunch: Cheddar-Garlic Biscuits
Snack: Simple Crab Rangoon
Dinner: Marinara Chicken with Cheeses
Dessert: Delicious Berry Cheese Cake

Day 4:
Breakfast: Poached Eggs with Whole Grain Avocado
Lunch: Irresistible Carrots
Snack: Garlic Buffalo Chicken Meatballs
Dinner: Delicious Fish and Chips
Dessert: Irresistible Cherry Pie

Day 5:
Breakfast: Simple Strawberry Breakfast Tarts
Lunch: Perfect Polenta Muffins
Snack: Fried Black Bean Corn Dip
Dinner: Beef Taco Chimichangas
Dessert: Great Funnel Cake

Day 6:
Breakfast: Asparagus and Pepper Strata Sandwich
Lunch: Butter Fried Cabbage
Snack: Fried Cinnamon and Sugar Peaches
Dinner: Buttermilk Fried Chicken
Dessert: Easy and Delicious Apple Fries

Day 7:
Breakfast: Baked Egg and Mushroom Cups with Baby Spinach
Lunch: Tasty Bagel Brussels Sprouts
Snack: Mexican Fried Potato Skins
Dinner: Tasty Cajun Prawn and Veggies
Dessert: Irresistible Honey-Roasted Pears

Week 4

Day 1:
Breakfast: Tasty Three-Berry Dutch Pancake
Lunch: Flavourful Courgette Fries
Snack: Prosciutto-Wrapped Asparagus
Dinner: Beef and Mushroom Calzones
Dessert: Sweet Pineapple Cheese Wontons

Day 2:
Breakfast: Cinnamon Crunchy Granola
Lunch: Delicious Street Corn
Snack: Bacon Jalapeño Cheese Bread
Dinner: Turkey Burgers
Dessert: Gorgeous Marble Cheesecake

Day 3:
Breakfast: Cranberry and Bran Flake Muffins
Lunch: Parmesan Cermini Mushrooms
Snack: Fried Cinnamon Apple Chips
Dinner: Classic Crab Cakes
Dessert: Fresh and Bright Orange Cheesecake

Day 4:
Breakfast: Mushroom-and-Tomato Stuffed Hash
Lunch: Easy Sweet Butternut Squash
Snack: Roasted Avocado Shishito Peppers
Dinner: Roast Beef
Dessert: Perfect Beignets

Day 5:
Breakfast: Simple Whole Wheat Banana-Walnut Bread
Lunch: Great Southwest-Style Corn Cobs
Snack: Courgette Chips
Dinner: Chicken Cordon Bleu
Dessert: Unbeatable Gooey Lemon Bars

Day 6:
Breakfast: Fried Salmon and Brown Rice Frittata
Lunch: Broccoli with Twice-baked Potatoes
Snack: Simple Bacon-Wrapped Jumbo Prawn
Dinner: Popular Fried Garlic Prawns
Dessert: Simple Blueberry Hand Pies

Day 7:
Breakfast: Cheddar Cheese and Buffalo Egg Cups
Lunch: Green Tomatoes
Snack: Spicy and Sweet Chicken Wings
Dinner: Swedish Meatballs
Dessert: Wonderful Big Chocolate Cookie

Poached Eggs with Whole Grain Avocado

Prep Time: 5 minutes| **Cook Time:** 7 minutes| **Serves:** 4

Olive oil cooking spray
4 large eggs
Salt
Black pepper
4 pieces whole grain bread
1 avocado
Red pepper flakes (optional)

1. Preheat the air fryer to 160 °C. Lightly coat the inside of four small oven-safe ramekins with olive oil cooking spray. 2. Crack one egg into each ramekin, and season with salt and black pepper. 3. Place the ramekins into the air fryer basket. Close and set the timer to 7 minutes. 4. While the eggs are cooking, toast the bread in a toaster. 5. Slice the avocado in half lengthwise, remove the pit, and scoop the flesh into a small bowl. Season with salt, black pepper, and red pepper flakes, if desired. Using a fork, smash the avocado lightly. 6. Spread a quarter of the smashed avocado evenly over each slice of toast. 7. Remove the eggs from the air fryer, and gently spoon one onto each slice of avocado toast before serving.
Per Serving: Calories 140; Fat 11.99g; Sodium 13mg; Carbs 5.9g; Fibre 3.5g; Sugar 1.02g; Protein 3.91g

Simple Red Pepper and Feta Frittata

Prep Time: 10 minutes| **Cook Time:** 20 minutes| **Serves:** 4

Olive oil cooking spray
8 large eggs
1 medium red pepper, diced
½ teaspoon salt
½ teaspoon black pepper
1 garlic clove, minced
120 g feta, divided

1. Preheat the air fryer to 180 °C. Lightly coat the inside of a 15-cm round cake pan with olive oil cooking spray. 2. Beat the eggs for 1 to 2 minutes, or until well combined in a large bowl. 3. Add the pepper, salt, black pepper, and garlic to the eggs, and mix together until the pepper is distributed throughout. 4. Fold in 60 g of the feta cheese. 5. Pour the egg-pepper mixture into the prepared cake pan, and sprinkle the remaining 60 g of feta over the top. 6. Place the pan into the preheated air fryer and bake for 18 to 20 minutes, or until the eggs are set in the centre. 7. Remove from the air fryer and allow to cool for 5 minutes before serving.
Per Serving: Calories 171; Fat 13.18g; Sodium 480mg; Carbs 4.28g; Fibre 0.7g; Sugar 2.22g; Protein 8.44g

Caprese Breakfast Pizza with Mozzarella Pearls and Basil Leaves

Prep Time: 5 minutes| **Cook Time:** 6 minutes| **Serves:** 2

1 whole wheat pita
2 teaspoons olive oil
¼ garlic clove, minced
1 large egg
⅛ teaspoon salt
55 g diced tomato
30 g mozzarella pearls
6 fresh basil leaves
½ teaspoon balsamic vinegar

1. Preheat the air fryer to 195 °C. 2. Brush the top of the pita with olive oil, then spread the minced garlic over the pita. 3. Crack the egg into a small bowl or ramekin and season it with salt. 4. Place the pita into the air fryer basket, and gently pour the egg onto the top of the pita. Top with the tomato, mozzarella pearls, and basil. 5. Bake for 6 minutes. 6. Remove the pita pizza from the air fryer and drizzle balsamic vinegar over the top. 7. Allow to cool for 5 minutes before cutting into pieces for serving.
Per Serving: Calories 198; Fat 7.46g; Sodium 225mg; Carbs 28.56g; Fibre 5.2g; Sugar 1.06g; Protein 5.44g

Baked Egg and Mushroom Cups with Baby Spinach

Prep Time: 5 minutes| **Cook Time:** 15 minutes| **Serves:** 6

Olive oil cooking spray
6 large eggs
1 garlic clove, minced
½ teaspoon salt
½ teaspoon black pepper
Pinch red pepper flakes
200 g mushrooms, sliced
30 g fresh baby spinach
2 spring onions, white parts and green parts, diced

1. Preheat the air fryer to 160 °C. Lightly coat the inside of six silicone muffin cups or a six-cup muffin tin with olive oil cooking spray. 2. Beat the eggs, garlic, salt, pepper, and red pepper flakes in a large bowl for 1 to 2 minutes, or until well combined. 3. Fold in the mushrooms, spinach, and spring onions. 4. Divide the mixture evenly among the muffin cups. 5. Place into the air fryer and bake for 12 to 15 minutes, or until the eggs are set. 6. Remove and allow to cool for 5 minutes before serving.

Per Serving: Calories 173; Fat 4.97g; Sodium 212mg; Carbs 30.33g; Fibre 4.6g; Sugar 1.34g; Protein 6.67g

Spinach and Swiss Frittata with Black Pepper Mushrooms

Prep Time: 10 minutes| **Cook Time:** 20 minutes| **Serves:** 4

Olive oil cooking spray
8 large eggs
½ teaspoon salt
½ teaspoon black pepper
1 garlic clove, minced
60 g fresh baby spinach
100 g mushrooms, sliced
1 shallot, diced
110 g shredded Swiss cheese, divided
Hot sauce, for serving (optional)

1. To prepare, heat your air fryer to 180 °C in advance. Lightly spritz the inside of a 15 cm round cake pan with olive oil cooking spray. 2. Beat the eggs, salt, pepper, and garlic in a large bowl for 1 to 2 minutes, or until well combined. 3. Fold in the spinach, mushrooms, shallot, and 55 g of the Swiss cheese. 4. Pour the seasoned egg mixture into the prepared cake pan, and sprinkle the remaining 55 g of Swiss over the top. 5. Place into the air fryer and bake for 18 to 20 minutes, or until the eggs are set in the centre. 6. Remove from the air fryer and allow to cool for 5 minutes. Drizzle with hot sauce (if using) before serving.

Per Serving: Calories 262; Fat 14.02g; Sodium 334mg; Carbs 24.52g; Fibre 3.7g; Sugar 1.11g; Protein 13.07g

Whole Wheat Breakfast Pita

Prep Time: 5 minutes| **Cook Time:** 6 minutes| **Serves:** 2

1 whole wheat pita
2 teaspoons olive oil
½ shallot, diced
¼ teaspoon garlic, minced
1 large egg
¼ teaspoon dried oregano
¼ teaspoon dried thyme
⅛ teaspoon salt
2 tablespoons shredded Parmesan cheese

1. Preheat the air fryer to 195 °C. 2. Brush the top of the pita with olive oil, then spread the diced shallot and minced garlic over the pita. 3. Crack the egg into a suitable bowl or ramekin, and season it with oregano, thyme, and salt. 4. Place the pita into the air fryer basket, and gently pour the egg onto the top of the pita. Sprinkle with cheese over the top. 5. Bake for 6 minutes. 6. Allow the pita to cool for 5 minutes before cutting into pieces for serving.

Per Serving: Calories 126; Fat 8.52g; Sodium 312mg; Carbs 8.94g; Fibre 1.1g; Sugar 0.18g; Protein 4.18g

Savory Potato Hash

Prep Time: 15 minutes| **Cook Time:** 18 minutes| **Serves:** 6

2 medium sweet potatoes, peeled and cut into 2.5 cm cubes
½ green pepper, diced
½ red onion, diced
100 g mushrooms, diced
2 tablespoons olive oil
1 garlic clove, minced
½ teaspoon salt
½ teaspoon black pepper
½ tablespoon chopped fresh rosemary

1. To prepare, heat your air fryer to 195 °C. 2. Toss the sweet potato cubes, pepper, onion, mushrooms, olive oil, garlic clove, salt, black pepper, and the chopped fresh rosemary together in a large bowl until the vegetables are well coated and seasonings distributed. 3. Pour the vegetables into the air fryer basket, making sure they are in a single even layer. (If using a smaller air fryer, you may need to do this in two batches.) 4. Cook for 9 minutes, then toss or flip the vegetables. Cook for 9 minutes more. 5. Transfer to a serving bowl or individual plates and enjoy.

Per Serving: Calories 141; Fat 4.79g; Sodium 211mg; Carbs 24.73g; Fibre 3.7g; Sugar 3.89g; Protein 2.74g

Low-Calorie Baked Peach Oatmeal

Prep Time: 5 minutes| **Cook Time:** 30 minutes| **Serves:** 6

Olive oil cooking spray
165 g certified gluten-free rolled oats
480 ml unsweetened almond milk
85 g raw honey, plus more for drizzling (optional)
120 g nonfat plain Greek yogurt
1 teaspoon vanilla extract
½ teaspoon ground cinnamon
¼ teaspoon salt
230 g diced peaches, divided, plus more for serving (optional)

1. To prepare, heat your air fryer to 195 °C. Lightly spritz the inside of a 15 cm cake pan with olive oil cooking spray. 2. Mix together the oats, almond milk, honey, yogurt, vanilla, cinnamon, and salt in a large bowl until well combined. 3. Fold in 115 g of the peaches and then pour the mixture into the prepared cake pan. 4. Sprinkle the remaining peaches across the top of the oatmeal mixture. Bake in the air fryer for 30 minutes. 5. Allow to set and cool for 5 minutes before serving with additional fresh fruit and honey for drizzling, if desired.

Per Serving: Calories 221; Fat 4.97g; Sodium 138mg; Carbs 49.62g; Fibre 5.8g; Sugar 28.47g; Protein 8.33g

Whole-Wheat Blueberry Breakfast Cobbler

Prep Time: 5 minutes| **Cook Time:** 15 minutes| **Serves:** 4

40 g whole-wheat pastry flour
¾ teaspoon baking powder
Dash sea salt
120 ml low fat milk
2 tablespoons pure maple syrup
½ teaspoon vanilla extract
Cooking oil spray
75 g fresh blueberries
30 g plain store-bought granola

1. Whisk the flour, baking powder, and salt in a medium bowl. Add the maple syrup, milk, and vanilla extract, and gently whisk, just until thoroughly combined. 2. Preheat the unit by selecting BAKE, setting the temperature to 175 °C, and setting the time to 3 minutes. Select START/STOP to begin. 3. Spray a 15-by-5-cm round baking pan with cooking oil and pour the batter into the pan. Top evenly with the blueberries and granola. 4. Once the unit is preheated, place the pan into the basket. 5. Select BAKE, set the temperature to 175 °C, and set the time to 15 minutes. Select START/STOP to begin. 6. When the cooking is complete, the cobbler should be nicely browned and a knife inserted into the middle should come out clean. Enjoy plain or topped with a little vanilla yogurt.

Per Serving: Calories 109; Fat 1.36g; Sodium 55mg; Carbs 22.86g; Fibre 1.6g; Sugar 14.24g; Protein 2.48g

Simple Whole Wheat Banana-Walnut Bread

Prep Time: 10 minutes| **Cook Time:** 23 minutes| **Serves:** 6

Olive oil cooking spray
2 ripe medium bananas
1 large egg
60 g nonfat plain Greek yogurt
60 ml olive oil
½ teaspoon vanilla extract
2 tablespoons raw honey
120 g whole wheat flour
¼ teaspoon salt
¼ teaspoon baking soda
½ teaspoon ground cinnamon
30 g chopped walnuts

1. To prepare, heat your air fryer to 180 °C. Lightly coat the inside of an 20-by-10-cm loaf tin with olive oil cooking spray. (Or use two smaller loaf tins) 2. Mash the bananas with a fork in a large bowl. Add the egg, yogurt, olive oil, vanilla, and honey. Mix until well combined and mostly smooth. 3. Sift the whole wheat flour, salt, baking soda, and cinnamon into the wet mixture, then stir until just combined. Do not overmix. 4. Gently fold in the walnuts. 5. Pour into the prepared loaf tin and spread to distribute evenly. 6. Place the loaf tin in the air fryer basket and bake for 20 to 23 minutes, or until golden brown on top and a toothpick inserted into the centre comes out clean. 7. Allow the bread to cool for 5 minutes before serving.
Per Serving: Calories 237; Fat 12.6g; Sodium 296mg; Carbs 29.93g; Fibre 3.5g; Sugar 10.79g; Protein 4.06g

Fried Salmon and Brown Rice Frittata

Prep Time: 15 minutes| **Cook Time:** 15 minutes| **Serves:** 4

Olive oil, for greasing the pan
1 egg
4 egg whites
½ teaspoon dried thyme
75 g cooked brown rice
75 g cooked, flaked salmon
15 g fresh baby spinach
40 g chopped red pepper
1 tablespoon grated Parmesan cheese

1. Rub a 15 by 5 cm pan with a bit of olive oil and set aside. 2. Beat the egg, egg whites, and thyme in a small bowl until they are well mixed. 3. Stir together the brown rice, salmon, spinach, and red pepper in the prepared pan. 4. Pour the egg mixture over the rice mixture and sprinkle with the Parmesan cheese. 5. Air fry at 160 °C for about 15 minutes, or until the frittata is puffed and golden brown and serve.
Per Serving: Calories 57; Fat 2.84g; Sodium 106mg; Carbs 1.1g; Fibre 0.1g; Sugar 0.56g; Protein 6.36g

Avocado and Egg Burrito

Prep Time: 10 minutes| **Cook Time:** 3 to 5 minutes| **Serves:** 4

2 hardboiled egg whites, chopped
1 hardboiled egg, chopped
1 avocado, peeled, pitted, and chopped
1 red pepper, chopped
3 tablespoons low-sodium salsa, plus additional for serving (optional)
1 (30 g) slice low-sodium, low-fat American cheese, torn into pieces
4 low-sodium whole-wheat flour tortillas

1. Thoroughly mix the egg whites, egg, avocado, red pepper, salsa, and cheese in a medium bowl. 2. Flatten the tortillas on a work surface and evenly divide the filling among them. Fold in the edges and roll up. Secure the burritos with toothpicks if necessary. 3. Put the burritos in the air fryer basket at 200 °C for 3 to 5 minutes, or until the burritos are light golden brown and crisp. 4. Serve with more salsa (if using).
Per Serving: Calories 204; Fat 14.67g; Sodium 86mg; Carbs 12g; Fibre 3.6g; Sugar 6.04g; Protein 8.17g

Low-Calorie Blueberry Muffins

Prep Time: 10 minutes| **Cook Time:** 15 minutes| **Serves:** 6

Olive oil cooking spray
120 g unsweetened applesauce
85 g raw honey
120 g nonfat plain Greek yogurt
1 teaspoon vanilla extract
1 large egg
190 g plus 1 tablespoon whole wheat flour, divided
½ teaspoon baking soda
½ teaspoon baking powder
½ teaspoon salt
75 g blueberries, fresh or frozen
1. To prepare, heat your air fryer to 180 °C. Lightly coat the inside of six silicone muffin cups or a six-cup muffin tin with olive oil cooking spray. 2. Combine the applesauce, honey, yogurt, vanilla, and egg in a large bowl, and mix until smooth. 3. Sift in the flour, the baking soda, baking powder, and salt into the wet mixture, then stir until just combined. 4. Toss the blueberries with the remaining 1 tablespoon flour in a small bowl, then fold the mixture into the muffin batter. 5. Divide the mixture evenly among the prepared muffin cups and place into the basket of the air fryer. Bake for 12 to 15 minutes, or until golden brown on top and a toothpick inserted into the middle of one of the muffins comes out clean. 6. Then allow the muffins to cool for 5 minutes before serving.
Per Serving: Calories 184; Fat 1.63g; Sodium 303mg; Carbs 40.63g; Fibre 3.8g; Sugar 18.11g; Protein 4.63g

Parmesan Veggie Frittata

Prep Time: 10 minutes| **Cook Time:** 8 to 12 minutes| **Serves:** 4

75 g chopped red pepper
50 g minced onion
35 g grated carrot
1 teaspoon olive oil
6 egg whites
1 egg
80 ml low fat milk
1 tablespoon grated Parmesan cheese

1. Stir together the red pepper, onion, carrot, and olive oil in a 15 by 5 cm pan, and put the pan into the air fryer. Then cook for 4 to 6 minutes, shaking the basket once, until the vegetables are tender. 2. Meanwhile, beat the egg whites, egg, and milk in a medium bowl until they are combined. 3. Pour the egg mixture over the vegetables in the pan. Sprinkle with the Parmesan cheese and return the pan to the air fryer to bake at 175 °C for 4 to 6 minutes more, or until the frittata is puffy and set. 4. Cut into 4 wedges and serve.
Per Serving: Calories 92; Fat 4.2g; Sodium 146mg; Carbs 4.08g; Fibre 0.5g; Sugar 2.68g; Protein 8.97g

Simple Granola

Prep Time: 5 minutes| **Cook Time:** 40 minutes| **Serves:** 4

85 g rolled oats
3 tablespoons pure maple syrup
1 tablespoon sugar
1 tablespoon neutral-flavoured oil, such as refined coconut, sunflower, or safflower
¼ teaspoon sea salt
¼ teaspoon ground cinnamon
¼ teaspoon vanilla extract

1. Insert the crisper plate into the basket and the basket into the unit. To preheat the unit, select BAKE, setting the temperature to 120 °C, and setting the time to 3 minutes. Select START/STOP to begin. 2. Stir together the oats, maple syrup, sugar, oil, salt, cinnamon, and vanilla in a medium bowl until thoroughly combined. Transfer the granola to a 15-by-5-cm round baking pan. 3. Once the unit is preheated, place the pan into the basket. 4. Select BAKE, set the temperature to 120 °C and set the time to 40 minutes. Select START/STOP to begin. 5. After 10 minutes, stir the granola well. Resume cooking, stirring the granola every 10 minutes, for a total of 40 minutes, or until the granola is lightly browned and mostly dry. 6. When the cooking is complete, place the granola on a plate to cool. Store the completely cooled granola in an airtight container in a cool, dry place for 1 to 2 weeks.
Per Serving: Calories 230; Fat 6.1g; Sodium 148mg; Carbs 38g; Fibre 4.2g; Sugar 11g; Protein 6.6g

Fresh Mixed Berry Muffins

Prep Time: 15 minutes| **Cook Time:** 12 to 17 minutes| **Serves:** 8

165 g plus 1 tablespoon plain flour, divided
50 g granulated sugar
2 tablespoons light brown sugar
2 teaspoons baking powder
2 eggs
180 ml whole milk
80 ml safflower oil
145 g mixed fresh berries

1. Stir together 165 g of flour, the granulated sugar, brown sugar, and baking powder in a medium bowl until mixed well. 2. Whisk the eggs, milk, and oil in a small bowl until combined. Stir the egg mixture together with the dry ingredients just until combined. 3. Toss the mixed berries with the remaining 1 tablespoon of flour in another small bowl until coated. Gently stir the berries into the batter. 4. Double up 16 foil muffin cups to make 8 cups. 5. Insert the crisper plate into the basket and the basket into the unit. Preheat the unit by selecting BAKE, setting the temperature to 155 °C, and setting the time to 3 minutes. Select START/STOP to begin. 6. Once the unit is preheated, place 4 cups into the basket and fill each three-quarters full with the batter. 7. Select BAKE, set the temperature to 155 °C, and set the time for 17 minutes. Select START/STOP to begin. 8. After about 12 minutes, check the muffins. If they spring back when lightly touched with your finger, they are done. If not, resume cooking. 9. When the cooking is done, transfer the muffins to a wire rack to cool. 10. Repeat the steps with the remaining muffin cups and batter. 11. Let the muffins cool for 10 minutes before serving.
Per Serving: Calories 280; Fat 13.8g; Sodium 90mg; Carbs 33.54g; Fibre 1g; Sugar 12.32g; Protein 5.75g

Jalapeño Egg Cups

Prep Time: 10 minutes| **Cook Time:** 10 minutes| **Serves:** 2

4 large eggs
20g chopped pickled jalapeños
40 g full-fat cream cheese
60 g shredded sharp Cheddar cheese

1. Beat the eggs, then pour into four silicone muffin cups in a medium bowl. 2. Place jalapeños, cream cheese, and Cheddar in a large microwave-safe bowl. Microwave for 30 seconds and stir. Take a spoonful, approximately ¼ of the mixture, and place it in the centre of one of the egg cups. Repeat with remaining mixture. 3. Place egg cups into the air fryer basket. 4. Adjust the temperature to 160 °C and set the timer for 10 minutes. 5. Serve warm.
Per Serving: Calories 286; Fat 23.78g; Sodium 425mg; Carbs 10.39g; Fibre 0.1g; Sugar 6.49g; Protein 7.89g

Mushroom-and-Tomato Stuffed Hash

Prep Time: 10 minutes| **Cook Time:** 20 minutes| **Serves:** 4

Olive oil cooking spray
1 tablespoon plus 2 teaspoons olive oil, divided
100 g mushrooms, diced
1 spring onions, white parts and green parts, diced
1 garlic clove, minced
300 g shredded potatoes
½ teaspoon salt
¼ teaspoon black pepper
1 Roma tomato, diced
55 g shredded mozzarella

1. To prepare, heat your air fryer to 195 °C. Lightly spritz the inside of a 15 -cm cake pan with olive oil cooking spray. 2. Heat 2 teaspoons olive oil over medium heat in a small frying pan. Add the mushrooms, spring onion, and garlic, and cook for 4 to 5 minutes, or until they have softened and are beginning to show some colour. Remove from heat. 3. Meanwhile, combine the potatoes, salt, pepper, and the remaining tablespoon olive oil in a large bowl. Toss until all potatoes are well coated. 4. Pour half of the potatoes into the bottom of the cake pan. Top with the mushroom mixture, tomato, and mozzarella. Spread the remaining potatoes over the top. 5. Bake in the air fryer for 12 to 15 minutes, or until the top is golden brown. 6. Remove from the air fryer and allow to cool for 5 minutes before slicing and serving.

Per Serving: Calories 179; Fat 1.6g; Sodium 406mg; Carbs 36.54g; Fibre 5.6g; Sugar 2.24g; Protein 9.05g

Bagels with Everything

Prep Time: 10 minutes| **Cook Time:** 10 minutes| **Serves:** 2

60 g self-rising flour, plus more for dusting
120 g plain Greek yogurt
1 egg
1 tablespoon water
4 teaspoons everything bagel spice mix
Cooking oil spray
1 tablespoon butter, melted

1. Using a wooden spoon, stir together the flour and yogurt in a large bowl until a tacky dough forms. Lightly spread a thin layer of flour over a clean work surface and then transfer the dough onto the surface. Roll the dough into a ball. 2. Cut the dough into 2 pieces and roll each piece into a log. Form each log into a bagel shape, pinching the ends together. 3. Whisk the egg and water in a small bowl. Brush the egg wash on the bagels. 4. Sprinkle 2 teaspoons of the spice mix on each bagel and gently press it into the dough. 5. Insert the crisper plate into the basket and the basket into the unit. Preheat the unit by selecting BAKE, setting the temperature to 165 °C, and setting the time to 3 minutes. Select START/STOP to begin. 6. Once the unit is preheated, spray the crisper plate with cooking spray. Drizzle the bagels with the butter and place them into the basket. 7. Select BAKE, set the temperature to 165 °C, and set the time to 10 minutes. Select START/STOP to begin. 8. When the cooking is complete, the bagels should be lightly golden on the outside. Serve warm.
Per Serving: Calories 716; Fat 13.88g; Sodium 442mg; Carbs 119.53g; Fibre 8.9g; Sugar 12.39g; Protein 27.63g

Chicken Sausages with Black Pepper

Prep Time: 15 minutes| **Cook Time:** 8 to 12 minutes| **Serves:** 8

1 Granny Smith apple, peeled and finely chopped
50 g minced onion
3 tablespoons ground almonds
2 garlic cloves, minced
1 egg white
2 tablespoons apple juice
⅛ teaspoon freshly ground black pepper
450 g chicken breast mince

1. Thoroughly mix the apple, onion, almonds, garlic, egg white, apple juice, and pepper in a medium bowl. 2. Gently work the chicken breast into the apple mixture with your hands until combined. 3. Form the mixture into 8 patties. Put the patties into the air fryer basket and air fry at 165 °C for 8 to 12 minutes, or until the patties reach an internal temperature of 75 °C on a meat thermometer. 4. Serve.
Per Serving: Calories 119; Fat 4.04g; Sodium 43mg; Carbs 4.1g; Fibre 0.7g; Sugar 2.63g; Protein 12.56g

Carrot and Golden Raisin Muffins

Prep Time: 15 minutes| **Cook Time:** 12 to 17 minutes| **Serves:** 8

190 g whole-wheat pastry flour
1 teaspoon baking powder
65 g brown sugar
½ teaspoon ground cinnamon
1 egg
2 egg whites
180 ml almond milk
3 tablespoons safflower oil
55 g finely shredded carrots
45 g golden raisins, chopped

1. Combine the baking powder, flour, brown sugar, and cinnamon in a medium bowl, and mix well. 2. Combine the egg, egg whites, almond milk, and oil in a small bowl and beat until combined. Then stir the egg liquid mixture into the dry ingredients just until combined. Don't overbeat; some lumps should be in the batter—that's just fine. 3. Stir the shredded carrot and chopped raisins gently into the batter. 4. Double up 16 foil muffin cups to make 8 cups. Put 4 of the cups into the air fryer and fill ¾ full with the batter. 5. Air fry at 160 °C for 12 to 17 minutes or until the tops of the muffins spring back when lightly touched with your finger. 6. Repeat with the remaining muffin cups and the remaining batter. Cool the cooked muffins on a wire rack for 10 minutes before serving.
Per Serving: Calories 211; Fat 7.19g; Sodium 50mg; Carbs 33.67g; Fibre 3.1g; Sugar 15.16g; Protein 5.43g

Dried Fruit Beignets with Brown Sugar

Prep Time: 22 minutes| **Cook Time:** 5 to 8 minutes| **Serves:** 16

1 teaspoon active quick-rising dry yeast
80 ml buttermilk
3 tablespoons brown sugar
1 egg
190 g whole-wheat pastry flour
3 tablespoons chopped dried cherries
3 tablespoons chopped golden raisins
2 tablespoons unsalted butter, melted
Icing sugar, for dusting (optional)

1. Mix the yeast with 3 tablespoons of water in a medium bowl. Let it stand for 5 minutes, or until it bubbles. 2. Stir in the buttermilk, brown sugar, and egg until well mixed. 3. Stir in the pastry flour until combined. 4. With your hands, work the cherries and raisins into the dough. Let the mixture stand for 15 minutes. 5. Pat the dough into an 20 by 20 cm square and cut into 16 pieces. Gently shape each piece into a ball. 6. Drizzle the balls with the melted butter. Place them in a single layer in the air fryer basket so they don't touch. Cook these in batches. Air-fry at 165 °C for 5 to 8 minutes, or until puffy and golden brown. 7. Dust with icing sugar before serving, if desired.
Per Serving: Calories 65; Fat 1.91g; Sodium 17mg; Carbs 10.34g; Fibre 1.3g; Sugar 2.07g; Protein 2.4g

Tasty Three-Berry Dutch Pancake

Prep Time: 10 minutes| **Cook Time:** 12 to 16 minutes| **Serves:** 4

2 egg whites
1 egg
60 g whole-wheat pastry flour
120 ml low fat milk
1 teaspoon pure vanilla extract
1 tablespoon unsalted butter, melted
150 g sliced fresh strawberries
75 g fresh blueberries
60 g fresh raspberries

1. Use an eggbeater or hand mixer to quickly mix the egg whites, egg, pastry flour, milk, and vanilla in a medium bowl until well combined. 2. Grease the bottom of a 15 by 5 cm pan with the melted butter with a pastry brush. Immediately pour in the batter and put the basket back in the fryer. Air fry at 165 °C for 12 to 16 minutes, or until the pancake is puffed and golden brown. 3. Then remove the pan from the air fryer; the pancake will fall. Top with the strawberries, blueberries, and raspberries. 4. Serve immediately.
Per Serving: Calories 194; Fat 5.29g; Sodium 70mg; Carbs 30.12g; Fibre 3.9g; Sugar 16.79g; Protein 7.88g

Simple French Toast Sticks

Prep Time: 6 minutes| **Cook Time:** 10 to 14 minutes| **Serves:** 4

3 slices whole-wheat bread, each cut into 4 strips
1 tablespoon unsalted butter, melted
1 egg
1 egg white
1 tablespoon low fat milk
1 tablespoon sugar
150 g sliced fresh strawberries
1 tablespoon freshly squeezed lemon juice

1. Place the bread strips on a plate and drizzle with the melted butter. 2. Beat the egg, egg white, milk, and sugar in a shallow bowl. 3. Dip the whole-wheat bread into the egg mixture and place on a wire rack to let the batter drip off. 4. Air-fry half of the bread strips at 195 °C for 5 to 7 minutes, turning the strips with tongs once during cooking, until golden brown. Repeat with the remaining strips. 5. Mash the strawberries and lemon juice with a fork or potato masher in a small bowl. 6. Serve the strawberry sauce with the French toast sticks.
Per Serving: Calories 137; Fat 5.43g; Sodium 152mg; Carbs 15.77g; Fibre 2.2g; Sugar 5.27g; Protein 6.62g

Asparagus and Pepper Strata Sandwich

Prep Time: 10 minutes| **Cook Time:** 14 to 20 minutes| **Serves:** 4

8 large asparagus spears, trimmed and cut into 5 cm pieces
40 g shredded carrot
75 g chopped red pepper
2 slices low-sodium whole-wheat bread, cut into 1 cm cubes
3 egg whites
1 egg
3 tablespoons low fat milk
½ teaspoon dried thyme

1. Combine the asparagus, carrot, red pepper, and 1 tablespoon of water in a 15 by 5 cm pan. Bake the veggies in the air fryer at 165 °C for 3 to 5 minutes, or until crisp-tender. Drain well. 2. Add the bread cubes to the vegetables and gently toss. 3. Whisk the egg whites, egg, milk, and thyme in a medium bowl until frothy. 4. Pour the egg mixture into the pan. Bake the strata for 11 to 15 minutes, or until it is slightly puffy and set and the top starts to brown. 5. Serve.
Per Serving: Calories 100; Fat 3.42g; Sodium 151mg; Carbs 9.5g; Fibre 1.5g; Sugar 2.45g; Protein 7.64g

Milk and Pumpkin Donut Holes

Prep Time: 15 minutes| **Cook Time:** 14 minutes| **Serves:** 12

125 g whole-wheat pastry flour, plus more as needed
3 tablespoons packed brown sugar
½ teaspoon ground cinnamon
1 teaspoon baking powder
70 g canned no-salt-added pumpkin purée (not pumpkin pie filling)
3 tablespoons low fat milk, plus more as needed
2 tablespoons unsalted butter, melted
1 egg white
Icing sugar (optional)

1. Mix the pastry flour, brown sugar, cinnamon, and baking powder in a medium bowl. 2. Beat the pumpkin, milk, butter, and egg white in a small bowl until they are combined. Add the pumpkin mixture to the dry ingredients and mix until combined. Add more flour or milk to form a soft dough. 3. Divide the dough into 12 pieces. Form each piece into a ball with floured hands. 4. Cut a piece of parchment paper or aluminum foil to fit inside the air fryer basket but about 2.5 cm smaller in diameter. Poke holes in the paper or foil and place it in the basket. 5. Put 6 donut holes into the basket, leaving some space around each. Air-fry at 180 °C for 5 to 7 minutes, or until the donut holes reach an internal temperature of 95 °C and are firm and light golden brown. 6. Let cool for 5 minutes. Remove from the basket and roll in icing sugar, if desired. Repeat with the remaining donut holes and serve.
Per Serving: Calories 59; Fat 1.69g; Sodium 8mg; Carbs 9.86g; Fibre 9.86g; Sugar 2.24g; Protein 1.87g

Cranberry and Bran Flake Muffins

Prep Time: 15 minutes| **Cook Time:** 15 minutes| **Serves:** 8

60 g bran cereal flakes
125 g plus 2 tablespoons whole-wheat pastry flour
3 tablespoons brown sugar
1 teaspoon baking powder
240 ml low fat milk
3 tablespoons safflower oil or peanut oil
1 egg
55 g dried cranberries

1. Mix the cereal, pastry flour, brown sugar, and baking powder in a medium bowl. 2. Whisk the milk, oil, and egg in a small bowl until they are combined. 3. Stir the egg mixture into the dry ingredients until just combined. 4. Stir in the cranberries. 5. Double up 16 foil muffin cups to make 8 cups. Put 4 cups into the air fryer and fill each three-fourths full with batter. Air fry at 160 °C for about 15 minutes, or until the muffin tops spring back when lightly touched with your finger. 6. Repeat with the remaining muffin cups and batter. 7. Let cool on a wire rack for 10 minutes before serving.
Per Serving: Calories 176; Fat 7.85g; Sodium 68mg; Carbs 23.84g; Fibre 3g; Sugar 7.89g; Protein 4.81g

Cinnamon Crunchy Granola

Prep Time: 10 minutes| **Cook Time:** 5 minutes| **Serves:** 6

220 g pecans, chopped
75 g unsweetened coconut flakes
110 g almond slivers
45 g sunflower seeds
40 g golden flaxseed
40 g sugar-free chocolate chips
10 g granular sweetener
2 tablespoons unsalted butter
1 teaspoon ground cinnamon

1. Mix all ingredients in a large bowl. 2. Place the mixture into a 6 x 2 cm round baking dish. Place dish into the air fryer basket. 3. Adjust the temperature to 160 °C and set the timer for 5 minutes. 4. Allow to cool completely before serving.
Per Serving: Calories 429; Fat 39.21g; Sodium 205mg; Carbs 16.3g; Fibre 7.4g; Sugar 6.84g; Protein 9.19g

Crispy Ham Egg Cups

Prep Time: 5 minutes| **Cook Time:** 12 minutes| **Serves:** 2

4 (25 g) slices deli ham
4 large eggs
2 tablespoons full-fat sour cream
40 g diced green pepper
2 tablespoons diced red pepper
2 tablespoons diced white onion
60 g shredded medium Cheddar cheese

1. Place one slice of ham on the bottom of four baking cups. 2. Whisk eggs with sour cream in a large bowl. Stir in green pepper, red pepper, and onion. 3. Pour the egg mixture into ham-lined baking cups. Top with Cheddar. Place cups into the air fryer basket. 4. Adjust the temperature to 160 °C and set the timer for 12 minutes or until the tops are browned. 5. Serve warm.
Per Serving: Calories 174; Fat 10.64g; Sodium 623mg; Carbs 5.57g; Fibre 0.5g; Sugar 1.34g; Protein 13.85g

Cheddar Cheese and Buffalo Egg Cups

Prep Time: 10 minutes| **Cook Time:** 15 minutes| **Serves:** 2

4 large eggs
50 g full-fat cream cheese
2 tablespoons buffalo sauce
35 g shredded sharp Cheddar cheese

1. Crack eggs into two (10 cm) ramekins. 2. Mix cream cheese, buffalo sauce, and Cheddar in a small microwave-safe bowl. Microwave the sauce mixture for 20 seconds and then stir well. Add a spoonful into each ramekin on top of the eggs. 3. Place ramekins into the air fryer basket. 4. Adjust the temperature to 160 °C and set the timer for 15 minutes. 5. Serve warm.
Per Serving: Calories 320; Fat 23.4g; Sodium 553mg; Carbs 4.6g; Fibre 0.3g; Sugar 2.8g; Protein 21.8g

Veggie Cream Frittata

Prep Time: 15 minutes| **Cook Time:** 12 minutes| **Serves:** 4

6 large eggs
60 g heavy whipping cream
45 g chopped broccoli
40 g chopped yellow onion
40 g chopped green pepper

1. Whisk eggs and heavy whipping cream in a large bowl. Mix in broccoli, onion, and pepper. 2. Pour the egg-cream mixture into a 15 cm round oven-safe baking dish. Place the baking dish into the air fryer basket. 3. Adjust the temperature to 175 °C and set the timer for 12 minutes. 4. Eggs should be firm and cooked fully when the frittata is done. 5. Serve warm.
Per Serving: Calories 145; Fat 10.6g; Sodium 114mg; Carbs 2.2g; Fibre 0.5g; Sugar 1g; Protein 10g

Low-Calorie Honey-Apricot Granola with Greek Yogurt

Prep Time: 10 minutes| **Cook Time:** 30 minutes| **Serves:** 6

85 g rolled oats
65 g dried apricots, diced
30 g almond slivers
30 g walnuts, chopped
30 g pumpkin seeds
40 g hemp hearts
85 to 110 g raw honey, plus more for drizzling
1 tablespoon olive oil
1 teaspoon ground cinnamon
¼ teaspoon ground nutmeg
¼ teaspoon salt
2 tablespoons sugar-free dark chocolate chips (optional)
735 g nonfat plain Greek yogurt

1. To prepare, heat your air fryer to 125 °C. Line parchment paper over the air fryer basket. 2. Combine the oats, apricots, almonds, walnuts, pumpkin seeds, hemp hearts, honey, olive oil, cinnamon, nutmeg, and salt in a large bowl, mixing so that the honey, oil, and spices are well distributed. 3. Pour the mixture onto the parchment paper and spread it into an even layer. 4. Bake for 10 minutes, then shake or stir and spread back out into an even layer. Continue baking for 10 minutes more, then repeat the process of shaking or stirring the mixture. Bake for an additional 10 minutes before removing from the air fryer. 5. Allow the granola to cool completely before stirring in the chocolate chips (if using) and pouring into an airtight container for storage. 6. For each serving, top 120 g Greek yogurt with 60 g granola and a drizzle of honey, if needed.
Per Serving: Calories 171; Fat 8.19g; Sodium 157mg; Carbs 28.11g; Fibre 4g; Sugar 14.91g; Protein 5.27g

Simple Strawberry Breakfast Tarts

Prep Time: 15 minutes| **Cook Time:** 10 minutes| **Serves:** 6

2 refrigerated piecrusts
160 g strawberry preserves
1 teaspoon cornflour
Cooking oil spray
120 g low-fat vanilla yogurt
25 g cream cheese, at room temperature
3 tablespoons icing sugar
Rainbow sprinkles, for decorating

1. Place the piecrusts on a flat surface. Cut each piecrust into 3 rectangles with a knife or a pizza cutter, for 6 total. Discard any unused dough from the piecrust edges. 2. Stir together the preserves and cornflour in a small bowl. Mix well, ensuring there are no lumps of cornflour remaining. 3. Scoop 1 tablespoon of the strawberry mixture onto the top half of each piece of piecrust. 4. Fold the bottom of each piece up to enclose the filling. Using the back of a fork, press along the edges of each tart to seal. 5. Insert the crisper plate into the basket and the basket into the unit. Preheat the unit by selecting BAKE, setting the temperature to 190 °C, and setting the time to 3 minutes. Select START/STOP to begin. 6. Once the unit is preheated, spray the crisper plate with cooking oil. Working in batches, spray the breakfast tarts with cooking oil and place them into the basket in a single layer. Do not stack the tarts. 7. Select BAKE, set the temperature to 190 °C, and set the time to 10 minutes. Select START/STOP to begin. 8. When the cooking is complete, the tarts should be light golden brown. Let the breakfast tarts cool fully before removing them from the basket. 9. Repeat the steps for the remaining breakfast tarts. 10. Stir together the yogurt, cream cheese, and icing sugar in a small bowl. Spread the breakfast tarts with the frosting and top with sprinkles.
Per Serving: Calories 48; Fat 1.71g; Sodium 35mg; Carbs 6.93g; Fibre 0.2g; Sugar 6.1g; Protein 1.49g

Perfect Polenta Muffins

Prep Time: 5 minutes | **Cook Time:** 10 minutes | **Serves:** 12

60 g plain flour
85 g Polenta
50 g granulated sugar
½ teaspoon baking powder
55 g salted butter, melted
120 ml buttermilk
1 large egg

1. Preheat the air fryer to 175 °C. 2. In a container, whisk together flour, polenta, sugar, and baking powder. 3. Add butter, buttermilk, and egg to dry mixture. Stir until well combined. 4. Divide batter evenly among twelve silicone or aluminum muffin cups, filling cups about halfway. Working in batches as needed, put in the air fryer and cook them for 10 minutes until golden brown. 5. Let cool 5 minutes before serving.
Per Serving: Calories 83; Fat 3.19g; Sodium 853mg; Carbs 11.89g; Fibre 0.4g; Sugar 2.66g; Protein 1.59g

Popular Macaroni and Cheese

Prep Time: 5 minutes | **Cook Time:** 25 minutes | **Serves:** 4

240 g dry elbow macaroni
240 ml chicken stock
120 ml whole milk
2 tablespoons salted butter, melted
200 g sharp cheddar cheese, shredded, divided
½ teaspoon ground black pepper

1. Preheat the air fryer to 175 °C. 2. In a 15 cm baking dish, combine macaroni, stock, milk, butter, half the cheddar, and pepper. Stir to combine. 3. Put in the air fryer basket and cook them for 12 minutes. 4. Stir in remaining cheddar, then return the air fryer basket to the air fryer and cook them for 13 minutes more. 5. Stir macaroni and cheese until creamy. Let cool 10 minutes before serving.
Per Serving: Calories 355; Fat 14.34g; Sodium 918mg; Carbs 49.52g; Fibre 0.9g; Sugar 8.91g; Protein 25.05 g

Perfect Roasted Broccoli

Prep Time: 5 minutes | **Cook Time:** 8 minutes | **Serves:** 4

300 g Broccoli florets
2 tablespoons olive oil
½ teaspoon salt
¼ teaspoon ground black pepper

1. Preheat the air fryer to 180 °C. 2. In a medium bowl, put broccoli and drizzle with oil. Sprinkle with salt and pepper. 3. Put in the air fryer basket and cook them for 8 minutes, shaking the air fryer basket twice during cooking, until the edges are brown and the centre is tender. 4. Serve warm.
Per Serving: Calories 80; Fat 7.17g; Sodium 319mg; Carbs 2.69g; Fibre 2.3g; Sugar0.47g; Protein 2.75g

Easy Sweet Butternut Squash

Prep Time: 10 minutes | **Cook Time:** 15 minutes | **Serves:** 8

1 medium Butternut Squash, peeled and cubed
2 tablespoons salted butter, melted
½ teaspoon salt
1½ tablespoons brown sugar
½ teaspoon ground cinnamon

1. Preheat the air fryer to 205 °C. 2. In a container, put squash and add butter. Toss to coat. Sprinkle salt, brown sugar, and cinnamon over Squash and toss to fully coat. 3. Put squash in the air fryer basket and cook them for 15 minutes, shaking the air fryer basket three times during cooking, until the edges are golden and the centre is fork-tender.
Per Serving: Calories 23; Fat 1.95 g; Sodium 853mg; Carbs 1.5 g; Fibre 0.4 g; Sugar 1.09g; Protein 0.32g

Delicious Roasted Carrots

Prep Time: 5 minutes | **Cook Time:** 12 minutes | **Serves:** 4

455 g baby carrots
2 tablespoons dry ranch seasoning
3 tablespoons salted butter, melted

1. Preheat the air fryer to 180 °C. 2. Put carrots into a 15 cm round baking dish. Sprinkle carrots with ranch seasoning and drizzle with butter. Gently toss to coat. 3. Put in the air fryer basket and cook them for 12 minutes, stirring twice during cooking, until carrots are tender.
Per Serving: Calories 104; Fat 5.92g; Sodium 420mg; Carbs 11.81g; Fibre 4g; Sugar 4.38g; Protein 1.11g

Flavourful Sweet Roasted Carrots

Prep Time: 5 minutes | **Cook Time:** 12 minutes | **Serves:** 4

455 g baby carrots
55 g brown sugar
2 tablespoons salted butter, melted
¼ teaspoon garlic powder
½ teaspoon salt
¼ teaspoon ground black pepper

1. Preheat the air fryer to 180 °C. 2. Put carrots into a 15 cm round baking dish. 3. Mix brown sugar, butter, and garlic powder. Pour mixture over carrots and carefully stir to coat. Sprinkle with salt and pepper. 4. Put in the air fryer basket and cook them for 12 minutes, stirring three times during cooking, until carrots are tender.
Per Serving: Calories 127; Fat 4.02g; Sodium 853mg; Carbs 23.22g; Fibre 3.5g; Sugar 17.4g; Protein 1.01g

Sweet Brussels Sprouts

Prep Time: 5 minutes | **Cook Time:** 15 minutes | **Serves:** 4

455 g Brussels Sprouts, trimmed and halved
2 tablespoons olive oil
½ teaspoon salt
¼ teaspoon ground black pepper

1. Preheat the air fryer to 175 °C. 2. In a container, put Brussels sprouts and drizzle with oil. Sprinkle with salt and pepper. 3. Put in the air fryer basket and cook 15 minutes, shaking the air fryer basket three times during cooking. 4. Serve warm.
Per Serving: Calories 110; Fat 7.1g; Sodium 853mg; Carbs 10.42g; Fibre 4.4g; Sugar 2.64g; Protein 3.89g

Quick Yeast Rolls

Prep Time: 10 minutes | **Cook Time:** 75 minutes | **Serves:** 16

4 tablespoons salted butter
50 g granulated sugar
240 ml hot water
1 tablespoon quick-rise yeast
1 large egg
1 teaspoon salt
315 g flour, divided

1. In a microwave-safe bowl, microwave butter for 30 seconds until melted. Pour 2 tablespoons of butter into a container. Add sugar, hot water, and yeast. Mix until yeast is dissolved. 2. Using a rubber spatula, mix in egg, salt, and 280 g flour. Dough will be very sticky. 3. Cover bowl with plastic wrap and let rise in a warm put for 1 hour. 4. Sprinkle the remaining 30 g flour on dough and turn onto a lightly floured surface. Knead 2 minutes, then cut into sixteen even pieces. 5. Preheat the air fryer to 175 °C. Spray a 15 cm round cake pan with cooking spray. 6. Sprinkle each roll with flour and arrange in pan. Brush with remaining melted butter. Put pan in the air fryer basket and cook them for 10 minutes until fluffy and golden on top. 7. Serve warm.
Per Serving: Calories 85; Fat 2.35g; Sodium 195mg; Carbs 13.75g; Fibre 0.5g; Sugar 13.12g; Protein 2.07g

Golden and Crispy Potato Balls

Prep Time: 15 minutes | **Cook Time:** 10 minutes | **Serves:** 4

460 g mashed potatoes (about 4 medium russet potatoes)
170 g sour cream, divided
1 teaspoon salt
½ teaspoon ground black pepper
100 g shredded sharp Cheddar cheese
4 slices bacon, cooked and crumbled
110 g panko bread crumbs

1. Preheat the air fryer to 205 °C. Cut parchment paper to fit the air fryer basket. 2. In a container, mix mashed potatoes, 115 g sour cream, salt, pepper, Cheddar, and bacon. Form twelve balls using 2 tablespoons of the potato mixture per ball. 3. Divide remaining 55 g sour cream evenly among mashed potato balls, coating each before rolling in bread crumbs. 4. Put balls on parchment in the air fryer basket and spritz with cooking spray. Cook them for 10 minutes until brown. 5. Serve warm.
Per Serving: Calories 252; Fat 15.37g; Sodium 815mg; Carbs 21.5g; Fibre 2g; Sugar 13.12g; Protein 7.5g

Lemon Butter Asparagus

Prep Time: 5 minutes | **Cook Time:** 15 minutes | **Serves:** 4

455 g asparagus, ends trimmed
55 g salted butter, cubed
Zest and juice of ½ medium lemon
½ teaspoon salt
¼ teaspoon ground black pepper

1. Preheat the air fryer to 190 °C. Cut a 15 cm × 15 cm square of foil. 2. Put asparagus on foil square. 3. Dot asparagus with butter. Sprinkle lemon zest, salt, and pepper on top of asparagus. Drizzle lemon juice over asparagus. 4. Fold foil over asparagus and seal the edges closed to form a packet. 5. Put in the air fryer basket and cook them for 15 minutes until tender. 6. Serve them warm.
Per Serving: Calories 93; Fat 7.82g; Sodium 853mg; Carbs 5.09g; Fibre 2.4g; Sugar 2.43g; Protein 2.65g

Classic Green Bean Casserole

Prep Time: 10 **minutes** | **Cook Time:** 20 minutes | **Serves:** 4

1 (250 g) can condensed cream of mushroom soup
60 g heavy cream
2 (360 g) cans cut green beans, drained
1 teaspoon minced garlic
½ teaspoon salt
¼ teaspoon ground black pepper
55 g packaged French fried onions

1. Preheat the air fryer to 160 °C. 2. In a 4-litre baking dish, pour soup and cream over green beans and mix to combine. 3. Stir in garlic, salt, and pepper until combined. Top with French fried onions. 4. Put in the air fryer basket and cook for 20 minutes until top is lightly brown and dish is heated through. 5. Serve warm.
Per Serving: Calories 110; Fat 6.27g; Sodium 853mg; Carbs 12.84g; Fibre 3.3g; Sugar 3.97g; Protein 2.89g

Great Southwest-Style Corn Cobs

Prep Time: 5 minutes | **Cook Time:** 15 minutes | **Serves:** 6

115 g sour cream
1½ teaspoons chili powder
Juice and zest of 1 medium lime
¼ teaspoon salt
6 mini corn cobs
120 g crumbled feta cheese

1. Preheat the air fryer to 175 °C. 2. Mix sour cream, chili powder, lime zest and juice, and salt. 3. Brush mixture all over corn cobs and put them in the air fryer basket. Cook them for 15 minutes until corn is tender. 4. Sprinkle with cotija.
Per Serving: Calories 221; Fat 5.81g; Sodium 853mg; Carbs 41.28g; Fibre 4.8g; Sugar 0.43g; Protein 8.01g

Delicious Garlic Bread

Prep Time: 10 minutes | **Cook Time:** 12 minutes | **Serves:** 6

130 g self-rising flour
245 g plain full-fat Greek yogurt
55 g salted butter, softened
1 tablespoon minced garlic
115 g shredded mozzarella cheese

1. Preheat the air fryer to 160 °C. Cut parchment paper to fit the air fryer basket. 2. In a container, mix flour and yogurt until a sticky, soft dough forms. Let sit 5 minutes. 3. Turn dough onto a lightly floured surface. Knead dough 1 minute, then replace to prepared parchment. Press out into an 20 cm round. 4. Mix Butter and garlic. Brush over dough. Sprinkle with mozzarella. 5. Put in the air fryer and cook them for 12 minutes until edges are golden and cheese is brown.
Per Serving: Calories 173; Fat 5.95g; Sodium 459mg; Carbs 19.47g; Fibre 0.9g; Sugar 3.22g; Protein 10.32g

Cheddar-Garlic Biscuits

Prep Time: 5 minutes | **Cook Time:** 10 minutes per batch | **Serves:** 10

250 g plain flour
1 tablespoon baking powder
1 teaspoon salt
½ teaspoon garlic powder
170 g sour cream
170 g salted butter, melted, divided
100 g shredded cheddar cheese

1. Preheat the air fryer to 205 °C. 2. In a container, mix flour, baking powder, salt, garlic powder, sour cream, and 115 g butter until well combined. Gently stir in cheddar. 3. Using your hands, form dough into ten even-sized balls. 4. Put balls in the air fryer basket, working in batches as necessary. Cook them for 10 minutes until golden and crispy on the edges. 5. Remove biscuits from the air fryer and brush with the remaining melted butter to serve.
Per Serving: Calories 199; Fat 11.36g; Sodium 334mg; Carbs 21.24g; Fibre 0.7g; Sugar 0.19g; Protein 3.44g

Crispy Tater Tots

Prep Time: 15 minutes | **Cook Time:** 25 minutes | **Serves:** 4

960 g water
455 g russet potatoes, peeled
½ teaspoon salt
½ teaspoon ground black pepper

1. In a large saucepan over medium-high heat, bring the water to a boil. Add potatoes and boil about 10 minutes until a fork can be easily inserted into them. Drain potatoes and let cool. 2. Preheat the air fryer to 175 °C. 3. Grate potatoes into a container. Add salt and pepper and mix gently by hand. 4. Form potatoes into sixteen 1-tablespoon tater tot–shaped balls. Put tater tots in the air fryer basket and spray lightly with cooking spray. 5. Cook them for 15 minutes, shaking the air fryer basket halfway through cooking time, until crispy and brown. 6. Serve warm.
Per Serving: Calories 92; Fat 0.1g; Sodium 301mg; Carbs 21.02g; Fibre 1.6g; Sugar 0.99g; Protein 2.54g

Butter Fried Cabbage

Prep Time: 5 minutes | **Cook Time:** 9 minutes | **Serves:** 2

Oil, for spraying
½ head cabbage, cut into bite-size pieces
2 tablespoons unsalted butter, melted
1 teaspoon granulated garlic
½ teaspoon coarse sea salt
¼ teaspoon freshly ground black pepper

1. Line the air fryer basket with parchment and spray some oil on it. 2. Combine the cabbage, butter, garlic, salt, and black pepper in a container. 3.Transfer the cabbage to the air fryer basket prepared before and spray some oil on it. 4.Turn to 190 °C and cook for 5 minutes, toss, and cook for another 3 to 4 minutes.
Per Serving: Calories 136 ; Fat 10.23g; Sodium 625mg; Carbs 10.91g; Fibre 3g; Sugar 5.44g; Protein 2.62g

Versatile Cauliflower Tots

Prep Time: 15 minutes | **Cook Time:** 12 minutes per batch | **Serves:** 4

1 (250 g) steamer bag riced cauliflower
35 g Italian bread crumbs
30 g plain flour
1 large egg
75 g shredded sharp Cheddar cheese
½ teaspoon salt
¼ teaspoon ground black pepper

1. Cook cauliflower according to the package directions. Let cool, then squeeze in a cheesecloth or kitchen towel to drain excess water. 2.Turn on the air fryer and preheat it to 205 °C. Cut parchment paper to fit the air fryer basket. 3. In a container, mix drained cauliflower, bread crumbs, flour, egg, and cheddar. Sprinkle in salt and pepper, then mix until well combined. 4. Roll 2 tablespoons of mixture into a tot shape. Repeat to use all of the mixture. 5. Put tots on parchment in the air fryer basket, working in batches as necessary. Spritz with cooking spray. Cook them for 12 minutes, turning tots halfway through cooking time, until golden brown. 6. Serve warm.
Per Serving: Calories 345; Fat 8.14g; Sodium 1346mg; Carbs 58.81g; Fibre 2.26g; Sugar 17.25g; Protein 8.02g

Flavourful Courgette Fries

Prep Time: 5 minutes | **Cook Time:** 20 minutes | **Serves:** 4

3 large courgette, trimmed
2 teaspoons salt
2 large eggs, whisked
100 g grated Parmesan cheese
110 g panko bread crumbs
2 teaspoons Italian seasoning

1.Cut a courgette in half crosswise. Slice down the length of each half, then cut each new piece in half lengthwise, to make eight sticks. Repeat with the remaining courgette for a total of twenty-four sticks. 2. Spread courgette fries in a single layer on top of a paper towel and sprinkle with salt. The salt will help draw out excess moisture. Put more paper towels on top of courgette fries to absorb moisture. Let sit for 30 minutes, changing paper towels out halfway through time. 3. Preheat the air fryer to 205 °C. 4. Put eggs in a medium bowl. Put Parmesan, bread crumbs, and Italian seasoning in a zippered storage bag. Dip six fries into egg, then put into storage bag and shake to coat. Remove and repeat with remaining courgette. 5. Spritz fries with cooking spray and put in the air fryer basket, working in batches as necessary. 6. Cook them for 12 minutes until crisp and brown, turning halfway through cooking time. 7. Serve and enjoy.
Per Serving: Calories 163; Fat 9.56g; Sodium 1764 mg; Carbs 9.31g; Fibre 0.6g; Sugar 0.72g; Protein 9.62g

Crispy Baby Potatoes

Prep Time: 10 minutes | **Cook Time:** 15 minutes | **Serves:** 4

Oil, for spraying
450 g baby potatoes
50 g grated Parmesan cheese, divided
3 tablespoons olive oil
2 teaspoons granulated garlic
½ teaspoon onion powder
½ teaspoon salt
¼ teaspoon freshly ground black pepper
¼ teaspoon paprika
2 tablespoons chopped fresh parsley, for garnish

1. Line the air fryer basket with parchment and spray some oil on it. 2. Wash the potatoes, pat dry with paper towels, and put in a container. 3. Mix together 25 g of Parmesan cheese, the olive oil, garlic, onion powder, salt, black pepper, and paprika. Coat the potatoes with the mixture. 4. Transfer the potatoes to the air fryer basket prepared before and spread them out in an even layer. 5. Cook them at 205 °C for 15 minutes, and stir them after 7 to 8 minutes. 6. Sprinkle with the parsley and the remaining Parmesan cheese.
Per Serving: Calories 244; Fat 14.89g; Sodium 525mg; Carbs 22.45g; Fibre 2.7g; Sugar 0.96g; Protein 6.06g

Sweet Potato Bites

Prep Time: 10 minutes | **Cook Time:** 25 minutes | **Serves:** 4

Oil, for spraying
3 medium sweet potatoes, peeled and cut into 2.5 cm pieces
2 tablespoons honey
1 tablespoon olive oil
2 teaspoons ground cinnamon

1. Line the air fryer basket with parchment and spray some oil on it. 2. Toss together the sweet potatoes, honey, olive oil, and cinnamon until evenly coated.3. Put the potatoes in the air fryer basket prepared before. 4. Cook them at 205 °C for 25 minutes.
Per Serving: Calories 161; Fat 4.67g; Sodium 31mg; Carbs 29.77g; Fibre 3.5g; Sugar 15.15g; Protein 1.63g

Versatile Bacon Potatoes with Green Beans

Prep Time: 10 minutes | **Cook Time:** 25 minutes | **Serves:** 4

Oil, for spraying
900 g medium russet potatoes, quartered
85 g bacon bits
250 g fresh green beans
1 teaspoon salt
½ teaspoon freshly ground black pepper

1. Line the air fryer basket with parchment and spray some oil on it. 2. Put the potatoes in the air fryer basket prepared before, and top them with the bacon bits and green beans, then prinkle them with the salt and black pepper and spray with oil. 3. Cook them at 180 °C for 25 minutes, and stirring and spraying with oil after 12 minutes of cooking time, until the potatoes are easily pierced with a fork. 4. Serve warm.
Per Serving: Calories 305 ; Fat 7.1g; Sodium 966 mg; Carbs 50.05g; Fibre 6.4g; Sugar 1.96g; Protein 12.4g

Zest Fried Aasparagus

Prep Time: 5 minutes | **Cook Time:** 10 minutes | **Serves:** 4

Oil, for spraying
10 to 12 spears asparagus, trimmed
2 tablespoons olive oil
1 tablespoon granulated garlic
1 teaspoon chili powder
½ teaspoon ground cumin
¼ teaspoon salt

1. Line the air fryer basket with parchment and spray some oil on it. 2. Cut them in half if the asparagus are too long to fit easily in the air fryer. 3. Put the asparagus, olive oil, garlic, chili powder, cumin, and salt in a zip-top plastic bag, seal the bag, and toss them until evenly coated. 4. Put the asparagus in the air fryer basket prepared before. 5. Cook them at 200 °C for 10 minutes, flipping them halfway through.
Per Serving: Calories 79; Fat 8.19g; Sodium 185mg; Carbs 1.49 g; Fibre 0.5g; Sugar 0.18g; Protein 0.47g

Delicious Butternut Squash

Prep Time: 15 **minutes** | **Cook Time:** 17 minutes | **Serves:** 4

Oil, for spraying
1 Butternut Squash, cut into 2.5 cm cubes
1 tablespoon olive oil
1 tablespoon maple syrup
1 teaspoon ground cinnamon

1. Line the air fryer basket with parchment and spray some oil on it. 2. Toss the squash with the olive oil, maple syrup, and cinnamon until evenly coated. 3. Put the squash in the air fryer basket prepared before. 4. Cook at 205 °C for 17 minutes, shaking and stirring after 9 minutes, until tender.
Per Serving: Calories 70; Fat 4.55g; Sodium 2mg; Carbs 7.97g; Fibre 1g; Sugar 3.81 g; Protein 0.38g

Popular Buffalo Cauliflower

Prep Time: 10 minutes | **Cook Time:** 30 minutes | **Serves:** 4

Oil, for spraying
1 head cauliflower, cut into florets
2 tablespoons unsalted butter, melted
1 tablespoon olive oil
120 ml buffalo sauce
50 g almond flour or plain flour
3 tablespoons dried parsley
1 tablespoon granulated garlic
1 teaspoon seasoned salt

1. Line the air fryer basket with parchment and spray some oil on it. 2. Put the cauliflower, melted butter, olive oil, and buffalo sauce in a zip-top plastic bag, seal, and toss. 3. Mix the almond flour, parsley, garlic, and seasoned salt in a bowl. 4. Add the cauliflower to the flour mixture, and combine to coat. 5. Put half of the cauliflower in the air fryer basket prepared before. 6. Cook at 175 °C for 15 minutes. After 7 or 8 minutes, shake and stir. 7. Do the same with the remaining cauliflower. 8. Serve warm.
Per Serving: Calories 214 ; Fat 8.95g; Sodium 973mg; Carbs 30.67g; Fibre 2.2 g; Sugar 13.24g; Protein 3.63g

Parmesan Cermini Mushrooms

Prep Time: 5 minutes | **Cook Time:** 15 minutes | **Serves:** 4

Oil, for spraying
450 g cremini mushrooms, stems trimmed
2 tablespoons olive oil
2 teaspoons granulated garlic
1 teaspoon dried onion soup mix
½ teaspoon salt
¼ teaspoon freshly ground black pepper
35 g grated Parmesan cheese, divided

1. Line the air fryer basket with parchment and spray some oil on it. 2. Toss the mushrooms with the olive oil, garlic, onion soup mix, salt, and black pepper until evenly coated. 3. Put the mushrooms in the air fryer basket prepared before. 4. Cook them at 185 °C for 13 minutes. 5. Sprinkle half of the cheese over the mushrooms and cook for 2 more minutes. 6. Transfer the mushrooms to a serving bowl, add the remaining Parmesan cheese, and toss until evenly coated.
Per Serving: Calories 442; Fat 11.32g; Sodium 459 mg; Carbs 87.11g; Fibre 13.1g; Sugar 2.53g; Protein 13.32 g

Broccoli with Twice-baked Potatoes

Prep Time: 10 minutes | **Cook Time:** 46 minutes | **Serves:** 4

Oil, for spraying
2 medium russet potatoes
1 tablespoon olive oil
20 g Broccoli florets
1 tablespoon sour cream
1 teaspoon granulated garlic
1 teaspoon onion powder
60 g shredded Cheddar cheese

1. Line the air fryer basket with parchment and spray some oil on it. 2. Wash the potatoes and pat dry with paper towels. Rub the outside of the potatoes with the olive oil and put them in the air fryer basket prepared before. 3. Cook them at 205 °C for 40 minutes. Let cool just enough to handle after cooking, then cut the potatoes in half lengthwise. 4. Put the Broccoli in a microwave-safe bowl, cover with water, and microwave on high for 5 to 8 minutes. Drain and set aside. 5. Scoop out most of the potato flesh and replace to a medium bowl. 6. Add the sour cream, garlic, and onion powder and stir until the potatoes are mashed. 7. Spoon the potato mixture back into the hollowed potato skins, mounding it to fit. Top with the broccoli and cheese. Return the potatoes to the air fryer basket. 8. Cook at 205 °C for 3 to 6 minutes until the cheese has melted. 9. Serve warm.
Per Serving: Calories 198 ; Fat 5.22g; Sodium 42mg; Carbs 34.61g; Fibre 2.6g; Sugar 1.39g; Protein 4.59g

Crispy Roasted Broccoli

Prep Time: 10 minutes | **Cook Time:** 15 minutes | **Serves:** 4

For Broccoli
Oil, for spraying
450 g broccoli florets
2 teaspoons peanut oil
1 tablespoon minced garlic
½ teaspoon salt
For Sauce
2 tablespoons soy sauce
2 teaspoons honey
2 teaspoons sriracha
1 teaspoon rice vinegar

1. Line the air fryer basket with parchment and spray some oil on it. 2. Toss together the Broccoli, peanut oil, garlic, and salt until evenly coated. 3. Spread out the Broccoli in an even layer in the air fryer basket. 4. Cook at 205 °C for 15 minutes, stirring halfway through. 5. In a small microwave-safe bowl, combine the soy sauce, honey, sriracha, and rice vinegar, and microwave them in the oven on high for about 15 seconds. Stir to combine. 6. Transfer the broccoli to a serving bowl and add the sauce. Gently toss and enjoy.
Per Serving: Calories 92 ; Fat 5.38 g; Sodium 449 mg; Carbs 8.83 g; Fibre 3.3g; Sugar 4.89g; Protein 4.31 g

Irresistible Carrots

Prep Time: 5 minutes | **Cook Time:** 12 minutes | **Serves:** 4

Oil, for spraying
385 g baby Carrots
3 tablespoons olive oil
1 tablespoon unsalted butter, melted
1 tablespoon honey
½ teaspoon salt
¼ teaspoon freshly ground black pepper
⅛ teaspoon dried dill, for garnish

1. Line the air fryer basket with parchment and spray some oil on it. 2. Toss the carrots, olive oil, butter, honey, salt, and black pepper in a medium bowl until evenly coated. 3. Put the carrots in the air fryer basket prepared before. 4. Cook the carrots at 200 °C for 12 minutes. 5. Transfer to a serving bowl, sprinkle with the dill, and enjoy.
Per Serving: Calories 167; Fat 13.4g; Sodium 349mg; Carbs 12.27g; Fibre 2.3g; Sugar 8.22g; Protein 0.93g

Delicious Street Corn

Prep Time: 10 minutes | **Cook Time:** 15 minutes | **Serves:** 4

Oil, for spraying
4 ears corn, shucked
60 g crumbled feta cheese
¼ teaspoon chili powder
¼ teaspoon salt
¼ teaspoon granulated garlic
⅛ teaspoon freshly ground black pepper
5 g chopped fresh coriander
1 tablespoon lime juice

1. Line the air fryer basket with parchment and spray some oil on it. 2. Put the corn in the air fryer basket. 3. Cook them at 200 °C for 10 minutes.4. Sprinkle the corn with the feta cheese and continue to cook for 5 more minutes. 5. Transfer to a serving plate and sprinkle with the chili powder, salt, garlic, black pepper, and coriander. Just before serving, drizzle with the lime juice.
Per Serving: Calories 40; Fat 3.21g; Sodium 237mg; Carbs 1.63g; Fibre 0.2g; Sugar 0.48g; Protein 1.5g

Crispy Okra

Prep Time: 5 minutes | Cook Time: 12 minutes **| Serves:** 6

Oil, for spraying
1 large egg
60 ml buttermilk
60 g plain flour
80 g polenta
½ teaspoon salt
¼ teaspoon freshly ground black pepper
450 g okra, trimmed and cut into slices

1. Preheat the air fryer to 205 °C. Line the air fryer basket with parchment and spray some oil on it. 2. Whisk the egg and buttermilk in a shallow bowl. 3. Mix together the flour, polenta, salt, and black pepper. 4. Toss the okra slices in the egg mixture, then dredge in the flour mixture until evenly coated, shaking off any excess. 5. Put the okra in the air fryer basket prepared before. For maximum crunch, spray some oil on it. 6. Cook them for 10 to 12 minutes, shaking and spraying with more oil after 4 minutes and after 7 minutes, until golden brown. 7. Sprinkle with additional salt as you like,.
Per Serving: Calories 131; Fat 2.08g; Sodium 221mg; Carbs 24.57g; Fibre 3.2g; Sugar 1.86g; Protein 4.27g

Super-Fast Green Bean Fries

Prep Time: 5 minutes **| Cook Time:** 5 minutes **| Serves:** 6

Oil, for spraying
450 g fresh green beans, trimmed
60 g plain flour
2 large eggs
110 g panko bread crumbs
50 g Parmesan cheese, plus more for serving (optional)
1 tablespoon granulated garlic

1. Line the air fryer basket with parchment and spray some oil on it. 2. Cut the green beans in half if any of the green beans are too long. 3. Put the green beans and flour in a zip-top plastic bag, seal, and shake well until evenly coated. 4. Whisk the eggs in a bowl. 5. Mix together the bread crumbs, Parmesan cheese, and garlic in another bowl. 6. Working in small batches, dip the green beans in the eggs, dredge in the panko mixture until evenly coated, and replace to the air fryer basket prepared before. 7.Cook them at 200 °C for 5 minutes. 8. Sprinkle with additional Parmesan cheese before serving as you like.
Per Serving: Calories 132 ; Fat 5.23g; Sodium 184 mg; Carbs 15.93g; Fibre 1.9g; Sugar 1g; Protein 5.8g

Healthy Kale Chips

Prep Time: 5 minutes **| Cook Time:** 5 minutes **| Serves:** 2

Oil, for spraying
80 g loosely packed stemmed and torn kale
2 tablespoons olive oil
2 tablespoons dry Ranch seasoning
¼ teaspoon salt

1. Line the air fryer basket with parchment and spray some oil on it. 2. Toss the kale, olive oil, Ranch seasoning, and salt until evenly coated. 3. Put the Kale in the air fryer basket. 4. Cook them at 185 °C for 4 to 5 minutes until crisp, shaking after 2 minutes. 5. Serve warm.
Per Serving: Calories 223; Fat 16.55g; Sodium 1001mg; Carbs 16.11g; Fibre 3.4g; Sugar 0.93g; Protein 4.14g

Tasty Bagel Brussels Sprouts

Prep Time: 15 minutes | **Cook Time:** 15 minutes | **Serves:** 8

Oil, for spraying
675 g Brussels Sprouts , trimmed
25 g grated Parmesan cheese
25 g finely chopped almonds
2 tablespoons olive oil
2 tablespoons Everything Bagel seasoning

1. Line the air fryer basket with parchment and spray some oil on it. 2. Bring a large pot of water to a boil over high heat. Add the brussels sprouts and cook until just softened, 8 to 10 minutes. Drain and let cool just long enough that you can handle them. 3. Cut the sprouts in half. Put the sprouts, Parmesan cheese, almonds, olive oil, and seasoning in a zip-top plastic bag, seal the bag, and toss until evenly coated. 4. Put the sprouts in the air fryer basket prepared before. 5. Cook them at 200 °C for 12 to 15 minutes, and stir after 6 to 8 minutes. 6. Serve immediately.
Per Serving: Calories 146; Fat 5.46g; Sodium 185mg; Carbs 20.03g; Fibre 4.2g; Sugar 3.37g; Protein 6.27g

Crunchy Roasted Edamame

Prep Time: 5 minutes | **Cook Time:** 10 minutes | **Serves:** 4

Oil, for spraying
185 g shelled Edamame
1 tablespoon olive oil
1 teaspoon hot sauce
½ teaspoon granulated garlic
Pinch salt, for serving

1. Line the air fryer basket with parchment and spray some oil on it. 2. In a medium bowl, toss together the edamame, olive oil, hot sauce, and garlic until evenly coated. 3. Put the Edamame in the air fryer basket. 4. Cook at 200 °C for 10 minutes and stir after 5 minutes, until crunchy. If you want the edamame to be even crunchier, cook for 5 more minutes. 5. Add some salt to taste as you like..
Per Serving: Calories 135; Fat 8.53g; Sodium 111mg; Carbs 7.91g; Fibre 4.1g; Sugar 1.75g; Protein 8.48g

Green Tomatoes

Prep Time: 5 minutes | **Cook Time:** 8 minutes | **Serves:** 4

Oil, for spraying
2 green (unripe) tomatoes, cut into slices
½ teaspoon salt
¼ teaspoon freshly ground black pepper
60 g plain flour
2 large eggs
120 ml buttermilk
110 g panko bread crumbs
160 g polenta
1. Turn on the air fryer and preheat it to 205 °C. Line the air fryer basket with parchment and spray some oil on it. 2. Season the tomato slices with salt and black pepper. 3. Put the flour on a shallow plate. 4. Whisk the eggs and buttermilk in a small bowl. 5. Combine the bread crumbs and polenta on another shallow plate. 6. Dredge the tomato slices in the flour, dip in the egg mixture, and coat with the panko bread crumbs on both sides. 7. Put the tomato slices in the air fryer basket and spray some oil on it. 8. Cook them for for 5 minutes, flip, and cook for 3 more minutes.
Per Serving: Calories 292; Fat 5.11g; Sodium 145mg; Carbs 52.36g; Fibre 2.9g; Sugar 2.68g; Protein 8.64g

Perfect Coconut Prawn

Prep Time: 15 minutes | **Cook Time:** 5 minutes | **Serves:** 4

1 (8-ounce) can crushed pineapple
115 g sour cream
80 g pineapple preserves
2 egg whites
85 g cornflour
55 g sweetened coconut
110 g panko bread crumbs
455 g uncooked large prawn, thawed if frozen, deveined and shelled
Olive oil for misting

1. Drain the crushed pineapple well, reserving the juice. 2. Combine the pineapple, sour cream, and preserves in a small bowl. Set aside. 3. In a shallow bowl, beat the egg whites with 2 tablespoons of the reserved pineapple liquid. Put the cornflour on a plate. Combine the coconut and bread crumbs on another plate. 4. Dip the prawn into the cornflour, shake it off, then dip into the egg white mixture and finally into the coconut mixture. 5. Put the prawn in the air fryer basket and mist with oil. Air-fry them for 5 to 7 minutes at 400 °F/ 205 °C.
Per Serving: Calories 352; Fat 4.67g; Sodium 782mg; Carbs 56.15g; Fibre 1.4g; Sugar 28.7g; Protein 20.16g

Easy Fish and Chips

Prep Time: 10 minutes | **Cook Time:** 20 minutes | **Serves:** 4

4 (100 g) fish fillets
Pinch salt
Freshly ground black pepper
½ teaspoon dried thyme
1 egg white
20 g crushed potato crisps
2 tablespoons olive oil, divided
2 russet potatoes, peeled and cut into strips

1. Pat the fish fillets dry and sprinkle with salt, pepper, and thyme. Set aside. 2. In a shallow bowl, beat the egg white until foamy. In another bowl, combine the potato chips and 1 tablespoon of olive oil and mix until combined. 3. Dip the fish fillets into the egg white, then into the crushed potato chip mixture to coat. 4. Toss the fresh potato strips with the remaining 1 tablespoon olive oil. 5. Use your separator to divide the air fryer basket in half, then fry the chips and fish at 205 °C. The chips will take about 20 minutes; the fish will take about 10 to 12 minutes to cook.
Per Serving: Calories 423; Fat 18.78g; Sodium 679mg; Carbs 37.4g; Fibre 2.9g; Sugar 1.22g; Protein 26.25g

Delicious Fried Prawn

Prep Time: 15 minutes | **Cook Time:** 15 minutes | **Serves:** 4

2 teaspoons Old Bay seasoning, divided
½ teaspoon garlic powder
½ teaspoon onion powder
½ teaspoon freshly ground black pepper
455 g large prawn, deveined, tails on
2 large eggs
1 teaspoon water
55 g panko bread crumbs
Extra-virgin olive oil, for spraying

1. Turn on and preheat the air fryer to 195 °C. 2. Mix in a medium bowl together 1 teaspoon Old Bay, the garlic powder, onion powder, and pepper. Add the prawns and toss to coat lightly. 3. Whisk in a small bowl the eggs with the water. 4. Mix the remaining 1 teaspoon Old Bay and the bread crumbs in a small shallow bowl. 5. Coat each prawn in the egg mixture, then the breading. 6. Sprinkle the air fryer basket with oil lightly. Put the prawns in a single layer in the air fryer basket. Do not overcrowd. Lightly spray with oil. 7. Air fry for 10 to 15 minutes, shaking the air fryer basket every 5 minutes.
Per Serving: Calories 134; Fat 4.71g; Sodium 668mg; Carbs 4.44g; Fibre 0.4g; Sugar 0.33g; Protein 17.32g

Tasty Cajun Prawn and Veggies

Prep Time: 10 minutes | **Cook Time:** 15 minutes | **Serves:** 6

455 g jumbo prawn, peeled and deveined
2 medium courgette, cut into 1 cm slices, then cut in half
2 peppers (red, yellow, or orange), cut into 2.5 cm chunks
2 tablespoons Cajun seasoning
2 tablespoons extra-virgin olive oil, plus more for the air fryer basket
2 fully cooked smoked turkey sausages, cut into 1 cm slices

1. Turn on and preheat the air fryer to 205 °C. 2. Toss in a large bowl the prawn, courgette, and peppers with the Cajun seasoning and olive oil. Stir in the smoked sausage slices. 3. Sprinkle the air fryer basket with oil lightly. Put the seasoned prawn, vegetables, and sausages in a single layer in the air fryer basket. 4. Air fry for 15 minutes, shaking the air fryer basket every 5 minutes until the vegetables are tender and seared..
Per Serving: Calories 137; Fat 5.93g; Sodium 904mg; Carbs 3.24g; Fibre 0.7g; Sugar 1.21g; Protein 16.45g

Delicious Bacon-Wrapped Scallops

Prep Time: 5 minutes | **Cook Time:** 10 minutes | **Serves:** 4

455 g jumbo sea scallops
455 g sliced bacon
Extra-virgin olive oil, for the air fryer basket
Freshly ground black pepper

1. Turn on and preheat the air fryer to 205 °C. 2. Pat the scallops dry with paper towels and remove any side muscles. 3. Cut the bacon slices in half so you have half a slice for each scallop. 4. Wrap each scallop in bacon and secure the bacon with a toothpick. 5. Sprinkle the air fryer basket with oil lightly. Put the bacon-wrapped scallops in a single layer in the air fryer basket. 6. Air fry for 8 minutes. Flip the scallops and season with pepper. Air fry for another 4 minutes until the scallops are tender and opaque.
Per Serving: Calories 599; Fat 46.63g; Sodium 1289mg; Carbs 7.44g; Fibre 0.1g; Sugar 0.94g; Protein 37.56g

Quick Lemon-Garlic Jumbo Scallops

Prep Time: 10 minutes | **Cook Time:** 10 minutes | **Serves:** 4

4 tablespoons unsalted butter, melted
2 tablespoons freshly squeezed lemon juice
1 tablespoon minced garlic
½ teaspoon salt
⅛ teaspoon freshly ground black pepper
455 g jumbo sea scallops
Extra-virgin olive oil, for the air fryer basket

1. Turn on and preheat the air fryer to 205 °C. 2. Combine the melted butter, lemon juice, garlic, salt, and pepper in a medium bowl. 3. Add the sea scallops and toss to coat. 4. Sprinkle the air fryer basket with oil lightly. Put the scallops in a single layer in the air fryer basket. 5. Air fry for 8 minutes, flipping after 4 minutes.
Per Serving: Calories 211; Fat 9.82g; Sodium 1053mg; Carbs 7.41g; Fibre 0.1g; Sugar 0.21g; Protein 23.92g

Great Garlic-Ginger Salmon

Prep Time: 10 minutes | **Cook Time:** 10 minutes | **Serves:** 4

60 ml soy sauce
2 tablespoons extra-virgin olive oil, plus more for the parchment paper
2 tablespoons grated fresh ginger
1 tablespoon minced garlic
1 tablespoon balsamic vinegar
4 (100 g) boneless, skinless salmon fillets

1. In a medium bowl, whisk the soy sauce, olive oil, ginger, garlic, and balsamic vinegar. 2. Put the salmon fillets in the marinade, then cover the bowl, and refrigerate them for at least 30 minutes but no longer than 3 hours. 3. Turn on and preheat the air fryer to 180 °C. 4. Put a sheet of air fryer perforated parchment paper in the air fryer basket and lightly spray with oil. Put the marinated salmon fillets in a single layer in the air fryer basket. 5. Air fry the salmon fillets for 6 minutes; flip the fillets and air fry for an another 4 to 6 minutes until they have an internal temperature of 60 °C.
Per Serving: Calories 129; Fat 8.46g; Sodium 1083mg; Carbs 8.84g; Fibre 0.7g; Sugar 2.5g; Protein 4.73g

Delicious Fish and Chips

Prep Time: 25 minutes | **Cook Time:** 35 minutes | **Serves:** 4

For Chips
2 large russet potatoes, scrubbed
1 tablespoon extra-virgin olive oil, plus more for greasing the air fryer basket
1 teaspoon seasoned salt
½ teaspoon freshly ground black pepper
For Fish
4 (100 g) white fish fillets, such as pollock, cod, or haddock
1½ teaspoons salt, divided, plus more for seasoning
1½ teaspoons black pepper, divided, plus more for seasoning
60 g plain flour
2 large eggs
1 teaspoon water
160 g panko bread crumbs
¼ teaspoon cayenne pepper
Extra-virgin olive oil, for spraying

1. Turn on and preheat the air fryer to 205 °C. 2. Cut the potatoes lengthwise into 1 cm thick slices and then again into 1-cm-thick fries. 3. Mix in a large bowl the olive oil with the seasoned salt and pepper, then add the fries and toss to coat. 4. Sprinkle the air fryer basket with oil lightly. Put the fries in a single layer in the air fryer basket. 5. Air fry them for 5 minutes; shake the air fryer basket and air fry for another 5 to 10 minutes. Set aside and keep warm. 6. Season the fish fillets with salt and black pepper. 7. Mix in a small shallow bowl together the flour, ½ teaspoon salt, and ½ teaspoon black pepper. 8. In a second shallow bowl, whisk together the eggs and a pinch each of salt and black pepper. 9. Combine in another bowl the bread crumbs, cayenne pepper, remaining 1 teaspoon salt, and remaining 1 teaspoon black pepper. 10. Turn on and preheat the air fryer to 205 °C. 11. Coat each fillet in the seasoned flour, then in the egg, then in the breading. 12. Sprinkle the air fryer basket with oil lightly. Put the coated fillets in a single layer in the air fryer basket. Lightly spray with oil. 13. Air fry them for 8 to 10 minutes; flip the fillets and lightly spray with oil, and air fry them for an another 5 to 10 minutes.
Per Serving: Calories 455; Fat 11. 27g; Sodium 1595mg; Carbs 53.02g; Fibre 3.6g; Sugar 2g; Protein 34.88g

Sophisticated Fish Sticks

Prep Time: 10 minutes | **Cook Time:** 15 minutes | **Serves:** 4

For Tartar Sauce
440 g mayonnaise
2 tablespoons dill pickle relish
1 tablespoon dried minced onions
For Fish Sticks
Oil, for spraying
450 g tilapia fillets
60 g plain flour
215 g panko bread crumbs
2 tablespoons Creole seasoning
2 teaspoons granulated garlic
1 teaspoon onion powder
½ teaspoon salt
¼ teaspoon freshly ground black pepper
1 large egg

1. Whisk the mayonnaise, pickle relish, and onions in a small bowl. Cover the bowl with plastic wrap and refrigerate them until ready to serve. You can make this sauce ahead of time, the flavours will intensify as it chills.2. Turn on and preheat the air fryer to 175 °C. Line the air fryer basket with parchment and sprinkle with oil lightly. 3. Cut the fillets into equal-size sticks and place them in a zip-top plastic bag. 4. Add the flour to the bag, seal, and shake well until evenly coated. 5. Mix the bread crumbs, Creole seasoning, garlic, onion powder, salt, and black pepper in a shallow bowl. 6. Whisk the egg in a small bowl. 7. Dip the fish sticks in the egg, then dredge in the bread crumb mixture until completely coated. 8. Put the fish sticks in the air fryer basket prepared before, and lightly sprinkle them with oil. Do not overcrowd. 9. Cook the fish sticks for 12 to 15 minutes until browned. Serve the dish with tartar sauce.
Per Serving: Calories 651; Fat 43.12g; Sodium 1735mg; Carbs 30.79g; Fibre 3.1g; Sugar 4.89g; Protein 34.16g

Classic Cod Nuggets

Prep Time: 15 minutes | **Cook Time:** 51 minutes | **Serves:** 4

4 (100 g) cod fillets
60 g plain flour
1 teaspoon seasoned salt
2 large eggs
1 teaspoon water
160 g panko bread crumbs
½ tablespoon dried parsley
1 teaspoon lemon-pepper seasoning
Extra-virgin olive oil, for spraying

1. Cut the cod fillets into 2.5 cm chunks. 2. Mix in a small shallow bowl together the flour and seasoned salt. 3. In a second small shallow bowl, whisk together the eggs and water. 4. In a third small shallow bowl, mix together the bread crumbs, parsley, and lemon-pepper seasoning. 5. Turn on and preheat the air fryer to 205 °C. 6. Coat each cod chunk in the seasoned flour, then in the egg, then in the breading. 7. Sprinkle the air fryer basket with oil lightly. Put the nuggets in a single layer in the air fryer basket. Lightly spray with oil.8. Air fry for 7 minutes. Flip the nuggets and lightly spray with oil. Air fry for an another 6 to 8 minutes.
Per Serving: Calories 378; Fat 19.29g; Sodium 1067mg; Carbs 26.81g; Fibre 6.1g; Sugar 1.52g; Protein 23.75g

Great Breaded Calamari

Prep Time: 15 minutes | **Cook Time:** 15 minutes | **Serves:** 4

455 g fresh calamari tubes, rinsed and patted dry
½ teaspoon salt, plus more for seasoning
½ teaspoon freshly ground black pepper, plus more for seasoning
125 g plain flour
3 large eggs
1 teaspoon water
110 g panko bread crumbs
2 teaspoons dried parsley
Extra-virgin olive oil, for spraying

1. Cut the calamari into ½ cm rings. Season with salt and pepper. 2. Combine the flour, salt, and pepper in a small bowl. 3. Beat the eggs with water in the second bowl. 4. Combine the bread crumbs and parsley in the third bowl. 5. Turn on and preheat the air fryer to 195 °C. 6. Coat the calamari rings in the seasoned flour, then in the egg, then in the breading. 7. Sprinkle the air fryer basket with oil lightly. Put the breaded calamari in a single layer in the air fryer basket. Lightly spray with oil.8. Air fry them for 10 to 15 minutes, shaking the air fryer basket a few times, until lightly browned and crispy.
Per Serving: Calories 465; Fat 5.48g; Sodium 439mg; Carbs 103.58g; Fibre 11g; Sugar 65.51g; Protein 7.13g

Fabulous Tuna Melt

Prep Time: 3 minutes | **Cook Time:** 10 minutes | **Serve:** 1 sandwich

Oil, for spraying
½ (125 g) can tuna, drained
1 tablespoon mayonnaise
¼ teaspoon granulated garlic, plus more for garnish
2 teaspoons unsalted butter
2 slices sandwich bread
2 slices cheddar cheese

1. Line the air fryer basket with parchment and sprinkle with oil lightly. 2. Mix in a medium bowl together the tuna, mayonnaise, and garlic. 3. Spread 1 teaspoon of butter on each slice of bread and place one slice butter-side down in the air fryer basket prepared before. 4. Put on the top a slice of cheese, the tuna mixture, another slice of cheese, and the other slice of bread, butter-side up. 5. Cook for 5 minutes at 205 °C, flip, and cook for 5 more minutes. 6. Sprinkle the sandwich with another garlic before cutting in half and serving.
Per Serving: Calories 540; Fat 35.46g; Sodium 880mg; Carbs 21.2g; Fibre 1.3g; Sugar 2.56g; Protein 34.28g

Glorious Tropical Tuna Steaks

Prep Time: 40 minutes | **Cook Time:** 10 minutes | **Serves:** 4

125 g crushed pineapple
70 g hoisin sauce
2 tablespoons freshly squeezed lime juice
1 tablespoon chopped coriander
2 teaspoons honey
1 teaspoon minced fresh ginger
1 teaspoon minced garlic
1 teaspoon extra-virgin olive oil, plus more for spraying
½ teaspoon sriracha
4 (150 g) ahi tuna steaks

1. Combine the pineapple, hoisin sauce, lime juice, coriander, honey, ginger, olive oil, and sriracha in a small bowl. 2. Put three-quarters of the marinade in a large zip-top bag and reserve the remaining marinade. Add the tuna steaks to the zip-top bag and coat them in the marinade. Seal the bag and refrigerate for 30 minutes. 3. Turn on and preheat the air fryer to 195 °C. 4. Remove the tuna steaks from the marinade and shake off any excess. 5. Sprinkle the air fryer basket with oil lightly. Put the tuna steaks in a single layer in the air fryer basket. Lightly spray with oil. 6. Air fry them for 5 minutes. Brush the reserved marinade on the tuna steaks, then let them rest for 5 minutes before slicing and serving.
Per Serving: Calories 263; Fat 2.54g; Sodium 336mg; Carbs 15.81g; Fibre 0.8g; Sugar 11.9g; Protein 42.27g

Flaky Chile-Lime Tilapia

Prep Time: 10 minutes | **Cook Time:** 15 minutes | **Serves:** 4

4 teaspoons chili powder
2 teaspoons ground cumin
2 teaspoons garlic powder
1 teaspoon salt
½ teaspoon freshly ground black pepper
4 (125 g – 150 g) tilapia fillets
Extra-virgin olive oil, for the parchment paper
2 limes, cut into wedges

1. Turn on and preheat the air fryer to 195 °C. 2. Combine in a small bowl the chili powder, cumin, garlic powder, salt, and pepper. 3. Pat the tilapia fillets dry with a paper towel. 4. Press the spice mixture all over the fish. 5. Line the air fryer basket with a sheet of perforated parchment paper, and lightly spray the parchment with oil. 6. Put the seasoned fillets in a single layer in the air fryer basket, leaving 1 cm of space between each to ensure even cooking. 7. Air fry the fillets for 10 to 15 minutes until flake easily. 8. Drizzle lime juice over the top, and enjoy.
Per Serving: Calories 144; Fat 3.75g; Sodium 722mg; Carbs 4.98g; Fibre 1.4g; Sugar 0.63g; Protein24.22g

Juicy Teriyaki Salmon

Prep Time: 6 minutes | **Cook Time:** 12 minutes | **Serves:** 4

4 (150 g) salmon fillets
120 ml soy sauce
55 g light brown sugar
2 teaspoons rice vinegar
1 teaspoon minced garlic
¼ teaspoon ground ginger
2 teaspoons olive oil
½ teaspoon salt
¼ teaspoon freshly ground black pepper
Oil, for spraying

1. Put the salmon the fillets in a small pan with skin-side up. 2. Whisk the soy sauce, brown sugar, rice vinegar, garlic, ginger, olive oil, salt, and black pepper in a small bowl. 3. Pour the mixture over the salmon fillets and marinate them for 30 minutes. 4. Line the air fryer basket with parchment and sprinkle with oil lightly. Put the salmon in the air fryer basket prepared before, skin-side down. 5. Cook the salmon fillets at 205 °C for 6 minutes, brush the salmon with more marinade, and cook for 6 more minutes.
Per Serving: Calories 607; Fat 24.4g; Sodium 975mg; Carbs 9.28g; Fibre 0.7g; Sugar 6.44g; Protein 82.27g

Amazing Coconut Prawn

Prep Time: 20 minutes | **Cook Time:** 10 minutes | **Serves:** 4

60 g plain flour
½ teaspoon salt
¼ teaspoon freshly ground black pepper
2 large eggs
Dash hot sauce
75 g sweetened shredded coconut
55 g panko bread crumbs
455 g large uncooked prawns, peeled and deveined
Extra-virgin olive oil, for spraying

1. Combine the flour, salt, and pepper in a small bowl. 2. In a second small shallow bowl, whisk together the eggs and hot sauce. 3. Combine the coconut and bread crumbs in the third bowl. 4. Turn on and preheat the air fryer to 185 °C. 5. Lightly coat the prawn in the flour mixture, then in the egg mixture, allowing the excess to drip off. Coat the prawn in the coconut breading. Press on the breading to ensure it adheres. 6. Sprinkle the air fryer basket with oil lightly. Put the coated prawn in a single layer in the air fryer basket. Lightly spray with oil. 7. Air fry the prawn for 5 minutes. Gently flip the prawn and lightly spray with oil, then air fry for another 4 to 5 minutes.
Per Serving: Calories 198; Fat 4.95g; Sodium 1052mg; Carbs 17.77g; Fibre 1.2g; Sugar 1.92g; Protein 19.24g

Simple Ranch Haddock Fillets

Prep Time: 10 minutes | **Cook Time:** 10 minutes | **Serves:** 4

60 g plain flour
½ teaspoon salt
½ teaspoon freshly ground black pepper
2 large eggs
160 g panko bread crumbs
2 tablespoons dry ranch dressing mix
4 (100 g) haddock fillets
Extra-virgin olive oil, for spraying

1. Combine the flour, salt, and pepper in a small bowl. 2. In a second small shallow bowl, whisk the eggs. 3. Combine the bread crumbs and ranch dressing mix in the third bowl. 4. Turn on and preheat the air fryer to 175 °C. 5. Lightly coat the haddock fillets in the flour mixture, then in the egg, allowing the excess to drip off. Coat the haddock pieces in the breading. Press on the breading to ensure it adheres. 6. Sprinkle the air fryer basket with oil lightly. Put the coated fillets in a single layer in the air fryer basket. Lightly spray with oil. 7. Air-fry the fillets for 8 minutes; gently flip the haddock fillets and lightly spray with oil, then air fry them for another 4 minutes.
Per Serving: Calories 304; Fat 8.19g; Sodium 838mg; Carbs 19.34g; Fibre 0.9g; Sugar 1.19g; Protein 35.75g

Healthy Fried Tilapia

Prep Time: 15 minutes | **Cook Time:** 6 minutes | **Serves:** 4

Oil, for spraying
110 g panko bread crumbs
2 tablespoons Old Bay seasoning
2 teaspoons granulated garlic
1 teaspoon onion powder
½ teaspoon salt
¼ teaspoon freshly ground black pepper
1 large egg
4 tilapia fillets

1. Turn on and preheat the air fryer to 205 °C. Line the air fryer basket with parchment and sprinkle with oil lightly. 2. Mix the bread crumbs, Old Bay, garlic, onion powder, salt, and black pepper in a shallow bowl. 3. Whisk the egg in a small bowl. 4. Coat the tilapia in the egg, then dredge in the bread crumb mixture until completely coated. 5. Put the tilapia in the air fryer basket prepared before. sprinkle with oil lightly. 6. Cook the fillets for 4 to 6 minutes until they have an internal temperature of 60 °C. .
Per Serving: Calories 166; Fat 4.61g; Sodium 397mg; Carbs 6.19g; Fibre 0.6g; Sugar 0.57g; Protein 24.98g

Healthy Fish Cakes

Prep Time: 10 minutes | **Cook Time:** 10 minutes | **Serves:** 4

2 (125 g) cans solid white albacore tuna in water, drained
1 large egg, beaten
160 g panko bread crumbs, divided
3 tablespoons finely chopped coriander
2 tablespoons sweet chili sauce
2 tablespoons oyster sauce
2 teaspoons minced garlic
¼ teaspoon cayenne pepper
½ teaspoon salt
½ teaspoon freshly ground black pepper
Extra-virgin olive oil, for spraying

1. Combine the tuna, egg, 80 g bread crumbs, coriander, chili sauce, oyster sauce, garlic, and cayenne pepper in a medium bowl. Stir the ingredients lightly with a fork until well mixed, but with some intact tuna chunks for texture. 2. Combine the remaining 80 g bread crumbs, the salt, and black pepper in small shallow bowl. 3. Turn on and preheat the air fryer to 195 °C. 4. Use a 50- to 75 g ice cream scoop to form the tuna mixture into equal-size patties. Coat each patty with the breading. 5. Sprinkle the air fryer basket with oil lightly. Put the fish cakes in a single layer in the air fryer basket. Lightly spray with oil. 6. Air fry for 4 minutes; gently flip the fish cakes and lightly spray with oil, and then air fry them for another 4 minutes.
Per Serving: Calories 185; Fat 5.33g; Sodium 1042mg; Carbs 10.06g; Fibre 1g; Sugar 1.7g; Protein 22.63g

Perfect Lemon Mahi-mahi

Prep Time: 5 minutes | **Cook Time:** 14 minutes | **Serves:** 2

Oil, for spraying
2 (150 g) mahi-mahi fillets
1 tablespoon lemon juice
1 tablespoon olive oil
¼ teaspoon salt
¼ teaspoon freshly ground black pepper
1 tablespoon chopped fresh dill
2 lemon slices

1. Line the air fryer basket with parchment and sprinkle with oil lightly. 2. Put the mahi-mahi in the air fryer basket prepared before. 3. Whisk the lemon juice and olive oil in a small bowl, then evenly brush the mahi-mahi with the mixture. 4. Sprinkle the mahi-mahi with the salt and black pepper and put on the top the dill. 5. Cook the mahi-mahi at 205 °C for 12 to 14 minutes 6. Replace the food to plates, and top each with one lemon slice. Enjoy.
Per Serving: Calories 349; Fat 24.92g; Sodium 709mg; Carbs 13.53g; Fibre 6.1g; Sugar 2.08g; Protein 20.31g

Indulgent Lobster Tails with Butter and Lemon

Prep Time: 10 minutes | **Cook Time:** 10 minutes | **Serves:** 2

2 lobster tails
Extra-virgin olive oil, for greasing the air fryer basket
2 tablespoons butter, melted, plus more for serving (optional)
Salt
1 lemon, cut into wedges

1. Turn on and preheat the air fryer to 205 °C. 2. Use kitchen scissors to cut the lobster tails from open end to the tail fins. Do not cut through the tail fins. Spread open the shell with your fingers and push the meat upward so it separates from the bottom shell. Leave the end attached at the tail fin. Hold the lobster meat up and push the shell together under the meat. Place the meat on the top of the shell. 3. Sprinkle the air fryer basket with oil lightly. Put the lobster tails in a single layer in the air fryer basket. Pour the melted butter over the lobster meat and season with salt. 4. Air fry them for 6 to 8 minutes until the lobster reaches an internal temperature of 60 °C. 5. Serve the dish with lemon wedges and extra melted butter (optional).
Per Serving: Calories 242; Fat 14.95g; Sodium 1889mg; Carbs 1.66g; Fibre 0.1g; Sugar 0.61g; Protein 24.98g

Great Cod with Creamy Mustard Sauce

Prep Time: 10 minutes | **Cook Time:** 5 minutes | **Serves:** 4

For Fish
Oil, for spraying
450 g cod fillets
2 tablespoons olive oil
1 tablespoon lemon juice
1 teaspoon salt
½ teaspoon freshly ground black pepper

For Mustard Sauce
120 g heavy cream
3 tablespoons Dijon mustard
1 tablespoon unsalted butter
1 teaspoon salt

1. Line the air fryer basket with parchment and sprinkle with oil lightly. 2. Rub the cod with the olive oil and lemon juice. Season with the salt and black pepper. 3. Put the cod fillets in the air fryer basket prepared before. 4. Cook the cod fillets at 175 °C for 5 minutes. Turn the temperature to 205 °C and cook for 5 more minutes, until they have an internal temperature of 60 °C.5. Add the heavy cream, mustard, butter, and salt to the saucepan, and bring to a simmer over low heat; then cook them for 3 to 4 minutes until the sauce starts to thicken.. 6. Replace the cod fillets to a serving plate, and drizzle with the mustard sauce. Enjoy.
Per Serving: Calories 476; Fat 36.18g; Sodium 1855mg; Carbs 11.81g; Fibre 7.5g; Sugar 1.53g; Protein 26.99g

Delicious Catfish Bites

Prep Time: 15 minutes | **Cook Time:** 20 minutes | **Serves:** 4

Oil, for spraying
450 g catfish fillets, cut into 5 cm pieces
240 ml buttermilk
80 g polenta
30 g plain flour
2 teaspoons Creole seasoning
125 g yellow mustard

1. Line the air fryer basket with parchment and sprinkle with oil lightly. 2. Put the catfish pieces and buttermilk in a zip-top plastic bag, then seal the bag, and refrigerate them for 10 minutes. 3. Mix in a shallow bowl together the polenta, flour, and Creole seasoning. 4. Remove the catfish pieces from the bag, and pat them dry with a paper towel. 5. Spread the mustard on all sides of the catfish, then dip them in the polenta mixture until evenly coated. 6. Put the catfish pieces in the air fryer basket prepared before, and lightly sprinkle them with oil. 7. Cook the catfish pieces at 205 °C for 10 minutes; flip them carefully, spray with oil, and cook for 10 more minutes. 8. Serve warm.
Per Serving: Calories 267; Fat 6.32g; Sodium 613mg; Carbs 27.14g; Fibre 2.4g; Sugar 3.71g; Protein 24.03g

Gorgeous Honey-Balsamic Salmon

Prep Time: 5 minutes | **Cook Time:** 8 minutes | **Serves:** 2

Oil, for spraying
2 (150 g) salmon fillets
60 ml balsamic vinegar
2 tablespoons honey
2 teaspoons red pepper flakes
2 teaspoons olive oil
½ teaspoon salt
¼ teaspoon freshly ground black pepper

1. Line the air fryer basket with parchment and sprinkle with oil lightly. 2. Put the salmon fillets in the air fryer basket prepared before. 3. Whisk the balsamic vinegar, honey, red pepper flakes, olive oil, salt, and black pepper in a small bowl, then brush the salmon fillets with the mixture. 4. Cook the salmon fillets at 200 °C for 7 to 8 minutes until they have an internal temperature of 60 °C. 5. Serve hot.
Per Serving: Calories 628; Fat 21.7g; Sodium 853mg; Carbs 23.12g; Fibre 0.2g; Sugar 22.15g; Protein 80.04g

Popular Fried Garlic Prawns

Prep Time: 15 minutes | **Cook Time:** 10 minutes | **Serves:** 3

For Prawns
Oil, for spraying
450 g medium raw prawns, peeled and deveined
6 tablespoons unsalted butter, melted
110 g panko bread crumbs
2 tablespoons granulated garlic
1 teaspoon salt
½ teaspoon freshly ground black pepper
For Garlic Butter Sauce
115 g unsalted butter
2 teaspoons granulated garlic
¾ teaspoon salt (omit if using salted butter)

1. Turn on and preheat the air fryer to 205 °C. Line the air fryer basket with parchment and sprinkle with oil lightly. 2. Put the prawns and melted butter in a zip-top plastic bag, seal the bag, and shake until evenly coated. 3. Mix the bread crumbs, garlic, salt, and black pepper in a medium bowl. 4. Add the prawns to the panko mixture and toss until evenly coated. Shake off any excess coating. 5. Put the prawns in the air fryer basket prepared before and sprinkle with oil lightly. 6. Cook the prawns for 8 to 10 minutes until golden brown and crispy, flipping and spraying them with oil after 4 to 5 minutes of cooking time. 7. Combine the butter, garlic, and salt in a microwave-safe bowl, and microwave them on 50% power for 30 to 60 seconds, stirring every 15 seconds. 8. Serve the prawns with the garlic butter sauce on the side for dipping.
Per Serving: Calories 490; Fat 39.46g; Sodium 2294mg; Carbs 9.89g; Fibre 0.6g; Sugar 0.74g; Protein 24.29g

Perfect Lemon Pepper Prawns

Prep Time: 15 minutes | **Cook Time:** 8 minutes | **Serves:** 2

Oil, for spraying
300 g medium raw prawns, peeled and deveined
3 tablespoons lemon juice
1 tablespoon olive oil
1 teaspoon lemon pepper
¼ teaspoon paprika
¼ teaspoon granulated garlic

1.Turn on and preheat the air fryer to 205 °C. Line the air fryer basket with parchment and sprinkle with oil lightly. 2. Toss in a medium bowl together the prawns, lemon juice, olive oil, lemon pepper, paprika, and garlic until evenly coated. 3. Put the prawns in the air fryer basket prepared before. 4. Cook the prawns for 6 to 8 minutes until pink and firm. 5. Serve hot.
Per Serving: Calories 216; Fat 10.86g; Sodium 965mg; Carbs 5.53g; Fibre 0.5g; Sugar 1.76g; Protein 23.75g

Delicious Prawns Kebabs

Prep Time: 15 minutes | **Cook Time:** 6 minutes | **Serves:** 4

Oil, for spraying
450 g medium raw prawns, peeled and deveined
4 tablespoons unsalted butter, melted
1 tablespoon Old Bay seasoning
1 tablespoon packed light brown sugar
1 teaspoon granulated garlic
1 teaspoon onion powder
½ teaspoon freshly ground black pepper

1.Line the air fryer basket with parchment and sprinkle with oil lightly. 2. Thread the prawns onto the skewers and place them in the air fryer basket prepared before. 3. Mix the butter, Old Bay, brown sugar, garlic, onion powder, and black pepper in a small bowl. Brush the sauce on the prawns. 4. Cook the prawns at 205 °C for 5 to 6 minutes until pink and firm. 5. Serve hot.
Per Serving: Calories 375; Fat 10.04g; Sodium 663mg; Carbs 56.22g; Fibre 0.3g; Sugar 13.12g; Protein 16.13g

Family Favorite Thai-style Prawns Stir-fry

Prep Time: 15 minutes | Cook Time: 15 minutes | **Serves:** 4

200 g fresh green beans
6 mini peppers, thinly sliced
2 tablespoons olive oil
455 g jumbo raw prawns, peeled and deveined
120 ml Thai stir-fry sauce
1 tablespoon minced garlic
315 g cooked jasmine or white rice
5 g shredded Thai basil

1. Toss together the green beans, peppers, and olive oil in an air fryer–safe pan. 2. Cook them at 175 °C for 5 minutes. 3. Add the prawns, stir, and cook for 5 more minutes. 4. Add the stir-fry sauce and garlic, stir, and cook for 5 more minutes. 5. Serve the dish over rice with a sprinkle of Thai basil on top.
Per Serving: Calories 338; Fat 9.67g; Sodium 1063mg; Carbs 32.69g; Fibre 2.7g; Sugar 4.48g; Protein 29.65g

Classic Crab Cakes

Prep Time: 10 minutes | Cook Time: 20 minutes | **Serves:** 4

2 large eggs
2 tablespoons mayonnaise
1 teaspoon Dijon mustard
1 teaspoon Worcestershire sauce
1½ teaspoons Old Bay seasoning
25 g finely chopped spring onions
450 g lump crabmeat
55 g panko bread crumbs
Oil, for spraying
1 lemon, cut into wedges

1. Mix the eggs, mayonnaise, mustard, Worcestershire sauce, Old Bay, and spring onions in a large bowl. 2. Add the crabmeat and bread crumbs and fold gently until combined. 3. Cover the bowl with plastic wrap and refrigerate for at least 1 hour. 4. Turn on and preheat the air fryer to 175 °C. Line the air fryer basket with parchment and sprinkle with oil lightly. 5. Divide the mixture into 8 equal portions and shape into 2.5 cm thick patties. Put 4 patties in the air fryer basket prepared before and sprinkle with oil lightly. 6. Cook the patties for 5 minutes, flip, spray with oil again, and cook for 5 more minutes. Do the same with the remaining patties. 7. Squeeze a lemon wedge over each crab patty.
Per Serving: Calories 80; Fat 6.01g; Sodium 112mg; Carbs 4.5g; Fibre 0.5g; Sugar 0.96g; Protein 2.4g

Easy French Mussels

Prep Time: 5 minutes | Cook Time: 8 minutes | **Serves:** 4

Oil, for spraying
455 g blue mussels
1 tablespoon unsalted butter
2 teaspoons minced garlic
1 teaspoon dried chives
1 teaspoon dried basil
1 teaspoon dried parsley
240 ml water
Lemon wedges, for garnish

1. Line the air fryer basket with parchment and sprinkle with oil lightly. 2. Run the mussels under cold water and, using a clean scrub brush, remove any debris. Lightly tap any open shells and toss those that don't close. 3. Combine the butter, garlic, chives, basil, parsley, and water in a microwave-safe bowl. Microwave them on high for 30 to 40 seconds; stir to combine and reserve half of the sauce in a small bowl. 4. Add the mussels to the remaining sauce and toss to coat. 5. Put the mussels in the air fryer basket prepared before. 6. Cook the mussels at 200 °C for 4 minutes, stir, and cook for another 4 minutes Discard any that do not open. 7. Replace to a serving bowl, drizzle with the reserved sauce, and garnish with lemon wedges.
Per Serving: Calories 130; Fat 5.64g; Sodium 327mg; Carbs 5.59g; Fibre 0.1g; Sugar 0.33g; Protein 13.8g

Flavourful Hot Crab Dip

Prep Time: 5 **minutes** | **Cook Time:** 12 minutes | **Serves:** 8

Oil, for spraying
100 g cream cheese, at room temperature
60 g sour cream
60 g mayonnaise
200 g lump crabmeat, fresh or frozen and thawed
60 g shredded cheddar cheese
1 tablespoon dry Italian seasoning
1 teaspoon finely chopped fresh parsley (optional)

1. Line an air fryer–safe ramekin or casserole-style dish with parchment and sprinkle with oil lightly. 2. Mix the cream cheese, sour cream, and mayonnaise. Fold in the crabmeat, cheese, and Italian seasoning in a small bowl. Replace to the prepared ramekin. 3. Cook them at 160 °C for 12 minutes. 4. Sprinkle with the parsley (if using) and serve warm.
Per Serving: Calories 154; Fat 11.57g; Sodium 274mg; Carbs 8.1g; Fibre 0.2g; Sugar 6.36g; Protein 154g

Easy Garlic Pesto Scallops

Prep Time: 5 **minutes** | **Cook Time:** 5 minutes | **Serves:** 4

Oil, for spraying
60 g basil pesto
3 tablespoons heavy cream
1 tablespoon olive oil
2 teaspoons minced garlic
1 teaspoon salt
½ teaspoon freshly ground black pepper
450 g sea scallops

1. Line the air fryer basket with parchment and sprinkle with oil lightly. 2. In a small saucepan, Combine the pesto, heavy cream, olive oil, garlic, salt, and black pepper in a saucepan, and bring to a simmer over medium heat, stirring occasionally, cook them for 2 minutes and set aside. 3. Put the scallops in the air fryer basket prepared before. 4. Cook the scallops at 160 °C for 5 minutes, flipping after 3 minutes to ensure both sides cook evenly. 5. Replace to a serving dish, pour the pesto sauce over the top.
Per Serving: Calories 237; Fat 14.36g; Sodium 686mg; Carbs 1.01g; Fibre 0.1g; Sugar 0.33g; Protein 26.37g

Delightful Crispy Fried Calamari

Prep Time: 10 **minutes** | **Cook Time:** 8 minutes | **Serves:** 4

Oil, for spraying
30 g plain flour
2 teaspoons salt, plus more if desired
2 teaspoons freshly ground black pepper
1 large egg
450 g calamari, cut into rings

1. Turn on and preheat the air fryer to 175 °C. Line the air fryer basket with parchment and sprinkle with oil lightly. 2. Combine the flour, salt, and black pepper in a zip-top plastic bag and set aside. 3. In a medium bowl, whisk the egg. Add the calamari and turn to coat evenly. 4. Replace the calamari to the zip-top bag, seal, and shake well until evenly coated. 5. Put the calamari in the air fryer basket prepared before and sprinkle with oil lightly. 6. Cook the calamari for 5 minutes; flip and spray with oil, and cook for another 3 minutes. 7. Sprinkle the dish with additional salt, if desired.
Per Serving: Calories 257; Fat 14.8g; Sodium 1251mg; Carbs 7.62g; Fibre 0.5g; Sugar 0.05g; Protein 23.41g

Distinct Cajun Prawns

Prep Time: 15 minutes | **Cook Time:** 9 minutes | **Serves:** 4

Oil, for spraying
450 g jumbo raw prawns, peeled and deveined
1 tablespoon Cajun seasoning
150 g cooked kielbasa, cut into thick slices
½ medium courgette, cut into ½ cm-thick slices
½ medium yellow squash, cut into ½ cm-thick slices
1 green pepper, seeded and cut into 2.5 cm pieces
2 tablespoons olive oil
½ teaspoon salt

1. Turn on and preheat the air fryer to 205 °C. Line the air fryer basket with parchment and sprinkle with oil lightly. 2. Toss the prawns and Cajun seasoning in a large bowl; mix in the kielbasa, courgette, squash, pepper, olive oil, and salt. 3. Replace the mixture to the air fryer basket prepared before. 4. Cook the prawns for 9 minutes, shaking the basket and stirring the prawns every 3 minutes. . 5. Serve hot.
Per Serving: Calories 291; Fat 16.93g; Sodium 1945mg; Carbs 4.06g; Fibre 0.5g; Sugar 0.83g; Protein 29.1g

Juicy Teriyaki Prawn Skewers

Prep Time: 10 minutes | **Cook Time:** 10 minutes | **Serves:** 4

455 g jumbo prawn, peeled and deveined
145 g teriyaki sauce
1 pineapple, peeled, cored, and cut into 2.5 cm chunks
Extra-virgin olive oil, for the air fryer basket

1. Turn on and preheat the air fryer to 205 °C. 2. Combine the prawn and teriyaki sauce in a medium bowl. 3. Thread the coated prawns and pineapple chunks in an alternating pattern onto 15 cm metal skewers. 4. Sprinkle the air fryer basket with oil lightly. Put the skewers in a single layer in the air fryer basket. 5. Air fry for 5 minutes, flipping the skewers and brush more teriyaki sauce onto the prawn, if desired. Air fry them for an another 5 minutes at 205 °C. 6. Serve hot.
Per Serving: Calories 193; Fat 2.72g; Sodium 1627mg; Carbs 15.38g; Fibre 0.5g; Sugar 14.07g; Protein 25.55g

Wonderful Fried Catfish

Prep Time: 10 minutes | **Cook Time:** 20 minutes | **Serves:** 4

240 ml buttermilk
4 catfish fillets
170 g polenta
1 tablespoon Creole seasoning
Extra-virgin olive oil, for spraying

1. Pour the buttermilk into a shallow baking dish. Put the catfish in the dish, cover, and refrigerate for at least 1 hour. 2. Turn on and preheat the air fryer to 205 °C. 3. Combine the polenta and Creole seasoning in a small bowl. 4. Take the catfish out of the dish and shake off any excess buttermilk. Put each fillet in the polenta mixture. Press on the polenta to ensure it adheres. 5. Sprinkle the air fryer basket with oil lightly. Put the coated catfish strips in a single layer in the air fryer basket. Lightly spray them with oil. 6. Air fry the catfish strips for 7 to 10 minutes; flip the catfish and lightly spray with oil, and air fry for an another 8 to 10 minutes. 7. When done, they should be golden brown and crispy.
Per Serving: Calories 338; Fat 6.83g; Sodium 342mg; Carbs 35.37g; Fibre 1.8g; Sugar 3.8g; Protein 30.96g

Chicken Patties

Prep Time: 15 minutes| **Cook Time:** 12 minutes| **Serves:** 4

455 g chicken thigh mince
55 g shredded mozzarella cheese
1 teaspoon dried parsley
½ teaspoon garlic powder
¼ teaspoon onion powder
1 large egg
50 g parmesan, grated

1. Mix chicken micne, mozzarella, parsley, garlic powder, and onion powder in a large bowl. Form them into four patties. 2. Place the four patties in the freezer for about 15–20 minutes until they are just about to firm up. 3. Whisk the large egg in a medium bowl. Add the parmesan to a large bowl. 4. Dip each chicken patty with the egg and press into parmesan until fully coated. Place the four patties evenly into the air fryer basket. 5. Adjust the temperature setting to 180 °C and set the timer for 12 minutes. 6. Patties will be firm and cooked to an internal temperature of 75 °C when done. Serve immediately.
Per Serving: Calories 202; Fat 7.37 g; Sodium 223 mg; Carbs 1.08 g; Fibre 0.3 g; Sugar 0.26 g; Protein 31.17 g

Greek Chicken Stir-Fry

Prep Time: 15 minutes| **Cook Time:** 15 minutes| **Serves:** 2

1 (150 g) chicken breast, cut into 2.5 cm cubes
½ medium courgette, chopped
½ medium red pepper, seeded and chopped
¼ medium red onion, peeled and sliced
1 tablespoon coconut oil
1 teaspoon dried oregano
½ teaspoon garlic powder
¼ teaspoon dried thyme

1. Place the chicken breasts, courgette, pepper, red onion, coconut oil, dried oregano, garlic powder, and the dried thyme into a large mixing bowl and toss until the coconut oil coats the meat and vegetables. Then pour the jichicken mixture from the bowl into the air fryer basket. 2. Adjust the temperature setting to 190 °C and set the timer for 15 minutes. 3. Shake the air fryer basket halfway through the cooking time to redistribute the food. Serve immediately.
Per Serving: Calories 215; Fat 14.73 g; Sodium 55 mg; Carbs 2.21 g; Fibre 0.5 g; Sugar 0.66 g; Protein 18.23 g

Chicken, Spinach, and Feta Bites

Prep Time: 10 minutes| **Cook Time:** 12 minutes| **Serves:** 4

455 g chicken thigh mince
70 g frozen spinach, thawed and drained
80 g crumbled feta
¼ teaspoon onion powder
½ teaspoon garlic powder
10 g grated parmesan

1. Mix the chicken thigh meat, spinach, feta, onion powder, garlic powder, and the parmesan in a large bowl. Roll the chicken-pork mixture into 5 cm and place evenly into the air fryer basket, working in batches if needed. 2. Adjust the temperature setting to 175 °C and set the timer for 12 minutes. 3. When done, internal temperature will be 75 °C. Serve immediately.
Per Serving: Calories 182; Fat 7.64 g; Sodium 234 mg; Carbs 1.46 g; Fibre 0.4 g; Sugar 0.61 g; Protein 25.69 g

Buffalo Chicken Cheese Sticks

Prep Time: 5 minutes| **Cook Time:** 8 minutes| **Serves:** 2

135 g shredded cooked chicken
60 ml buffalo sauce
115 g shredded mozzarella cheese
1 large egg
60 g crumbled feta

1. In a large bowl, mix the cooked chicken, buffalo sauce, mozzarella cheese, and then whisk the egg. Cut a suitable piece of parchment to fit your air fryer basket and press the mixture into a 1 cm thick circle. 2. Sprinkle the mixture with the crumbled feta cheese and place them into the air fryer basket. 3. Adjust the temperature setting to 205 °C and set the timer for 8 minutes. 4. Flip over the cheese mixture, when the cooking time passed 5 minutes. 5. Allow them to cool for 5 minutes before cutting into sticks. Serve warm.
Per Serving: Calories 334; Fat 9.44 g; Sodium 1030 mg; Carbs 17.5 g; Fibre 1.3 g; Sugar 13.58 g; Protein 43 g

Italian Chicken Thighs

Prep Time: 5 minutes| **Cook Time:** 20 minutes| **Serves:** 2

4 bone-in, skin-on chicken thighs
2 tablespoons unsalted butter, melted
1 teaspoon dried parsley
1 teaspoon dried basil
½ teaspoon garlic powder
¼ teaspoon onion powder
¼ teaspoon dried oregano

1. Brush the unsaltedd butter over chicken thighs and sprinkle the dried parsley, basil, garlic powder, onion powder, and the dried oregano over the thighs. Place thighs into the air fryer basket. 2. Adjust the temperature setting to 195 °C and set the timer for 20 minutes. 3. Halfway through the cooking time, flip the thighs. 4. When fully cooked, internal temperature will be at least 75 °C and skin will be crispy. Serve warm.
Per Serving: Calories 493; Fat 39.14 g; Sodium 159 mg; Carbs 1.6 g; Fibre 0.3 g; Sugar 0.06 g; Protein 31.96 g

Chicken Fajitas

Prep Time: 10 minutes| **Cook Time:** 10 to 14 minutes| **Serves:** 4

Cooking oil spray
4 boneless, skinless chicken breasts, sliced crosswise
1 small red onion, sliced
2 red peppers, seeded and sliced
120 ml spicy ranch salad dressing, divided
½ teaspoon dried oregano
8 corn tortillas
70 g torn butter lettuce leaves
2 avocados, peeled, pitted, and chopped

1. Insert the crisper plate into the basket and the basket into the unit. Preheat the unit by selecting BAKE, setting the temperature to 190 °C, and setting the time to 3 minutes. Select START/STOP to begin. 2. Once the unit is preheated, spray the crisper plate with cooking oil. Place the chicken, red onion, and red pepper into the basket. Drizzle with 1 tablespoon of the salad dressing and season with the oregano. Toss to combine. 3. Select BAKE, set the temperature to 190 °C, and set the time to 14 minutes. Select START/STOP to begin. 4. After 10 minutes, check the chicken. If a food thermometer inserted into the chicken registers at least 75 °C, it is done. If not, resume cooking. 5. When the cooking is complete, transfer the chicken and vegetables to a bowl and toss with the remaining salad dressing. 6. Serve the chicken mixture family-style with the tortillas, lettuce, and avocados, and let everyone make their own plates.
Per Serving: Calories 919; Fat 42.05 g; Sodium 1070 mg; Carbs 62.72 g; Fibre 10.1 g; Sugar 7.41 g; Protein 72.06 g

Chicken and Spinach Salad

Prep Time: 10 minutes| **Cook Time:** 20 minutes| **Serves:** 4

3 (125 g) boneless, skinless chicken breasts, cut into 2.5 cm cubes
5 teaspoons extra-virgin olive oil
½ teaspoon dried thyme
1 medium red onion, sliced
1 red pepper, sliced
1 small courgette, cut into strips
3 tablespoons freshly squeezed lemon juice
180 g fresh baby spinach leaves

1. Insert the crisper plate into the basket and the basket into the unit. Preheat the unit by selecting AIR ROAST, setting the temperature to 190 °C, and setting the time to 3 minutes. Select START/STOP to begin. 2. Combine the chicken, olive oil, and thyme in a large bowl. Toss to coat. Transfer to a medium metal bowl that fits into the basket. 3. Once the unit is preheated, place the bowl into the basket. 4. Select AIR ROAST, set the temperature to 190 °C, and set the time to 20 minutes. Select START/STOP to begin. 5. After 8 minutes, add the red onion, red pepper, and courgette to the bowl. Resume cooking. After about 6 minutes more, stir the chicken and vegetables. Resume cooking. 6. When the cooking is complete, a food thermometer inserted into the chicken should register at least 75 °C. Remove the bowl from the unit and stir in the lemon juice. 7. Put the spinach in a serving bowl and top with the chicken mixture. Toss to combine and serve immediately.
Per Serving: Calories 102; Fat 5.97 g; Sodium 108 mg; Carbs 3.73 g; Fibre 1.3 g; Sugar 1.17 g; Protein 9.06 g

Cajun Pepper & Chicken Kebabs

Prep Time: 20 minutes| **Cook Time:** 20 minutes| **Serves:** 6

Olive oil
775 g boneless, skinless chicken breasts, cut into bite-sized chunks
1½ tablespoons Cajun seasoning, divided
1 medium red pepper, cut into big chunks
1 medium green pepper, cut into big chunks
1 medium onion, cut into big chunks

1. Spray an air fryer basket lightly with olive oil. 2. Toss the chicken with 1 tablespoon of Cajun seasoning in a large bowl, and spray with olive oil to coat. 3. In a separate, large bowl, toss the peppers and onion with the remaining ½ tablespoon of Cajun seasoning, and spray with olive oil to coat. 4. If using wooden skewers, soak them in water for at least 30 minutes before using. 5. Thread the chicken chunks and vegetables onto the skewers, alternating with chicken, then vegetable. 6. Transfer the skewers to the air fryer basket in a single layer. You may need to cook them in batches. 7. Air fry at 175 °C for 10 minutes. Flip the skewers over and lightly spray with olive oil. Air fry until the chicken has an internal temperature of at least 75 °C, another 5 to 10 minutes.
Per Serving: Calories 152; Fat 4.24 g; Sodium 352 mg; Carbs 4.86 g; Fibre 1.1 g; Sugar 2.22 g; Protein 23.69 g

Chicken Taquitos

Prep Time: 15 minutes| **Cook Time:** 10 minutes| **Serves:** 6

Olive oil
200 g fat-free cream cheese, softened
30 ml Buffalo sauce
280 g shredded cooked chicken
12 (18 cm) low-carb flour tortillas

1. Spray an air fryer basket lightly with olive oil. 2. In a large bowl, mix together the cream cheese and Buffalo sauce until well-combined. Add the chicken and stir until combined. 3. Place the tortillas on a clean workspace. Spoon 2 to 3 tablespoons of the chicken mixture in a thin line down the centre of each tortilla. Roll up the tortillas. 4. Place the tortillas in the fryer basket, seam side down. Spray each tortilla lightly with olive oil. Cook the taquitos in batches as needed. 5. Air fry at 180 °C until golden brown, for 5 to 10 minutes.
Per Serving: Calories 283; Fat 8.02 g; Sodium 371 mg; Carbs 29.66 g; Fibre 2.8 g; Sugar 4.59 g; Protein 23.14 g

Black Pepper Chicken with Celery

Prep Time: 10 minutes| **Cook Time:** 15 minutes| **Serves:** 4

Olive oil
120 ml soy sauce
2 tablespoons hoisin sauce
4 teaspoons minced garlic
1 teaspoon freshly ground black pepper
8 boneless, skinless chicken tenderloins
120 g chopped celery
1 medium red pepper, diced

1. Spray an air fryer basket lightly with olive oil. 2. Mix together the hoisin sauce, garlic, soy sauce, and black pepper in a large bowl to make a marinade. Add the chicken, celery, and pepper and toss to coat. 3. Shake the excess marinade off the chicken, place it and the vegetables in the air fryer basket, and lightly spray with olive oil. Cook them in batches as needed. Reserve the remaining marinade. 4. Air fry at 190 °C for 8 minutes. Turn the chicken over and brush with some of the remaining marinade. Cook until the chicken reaches an internal temperature of at least 75 °C, an additional 5 to 7 minutes.
Per Serving: Calories 193; Fat 8.14 g; Sodium 658 mg; Carbs 15.29 g; Fibre 2.1 g; Sugar 9.95 g; Protein 14.23 g

Parmesan-crumb Chicken

Prep Time: 1 hour 10 minutes| **Cook Time:** 20 minutes| **Serves:** 4

1 egg
2 tablespoons lemon juice
2 teaspoons minced garlic
½ teaspoon salt
½ teaspoon freshly ground black pepper
4 boneless, skinless chicken breasts, thin cut
Olive oil
55 g whole-wheat bread crumbs
25 g grated Parmesan cheese

1. In a medium bowl, whisk together the egg, lemon juice, garlic, salt, and black pepper. Add the chicken breasts, cover, and refrigerate for up to 1 hour. 2. Combine the Parmesan cheese together with bread crumbs in a shallow bowl. 3. Spray an air fryer basket lightly with olive oil. 4. Remove the chicken breasts from the egg mixture, then dredge them in the bread crumb mixture, and place in the air fryer basket in a single layer. Lightly spray the chicken breasts with olive oil. You may need to cook the chicken in batches. 5. Air fry at 180 °C for 8 minutes. Flip the chicken over, lightly spray with olive oil, and cook until the chicken reaches an internal temperature of 75 °C, for an additional 7 to 12 minutes.
Per Serving: Calories 516; Fat 14.24 g; Sodium 789 mg; Carbs 12.2 g; Fibre 0.7 g; Sugar 1.27 g; Protein 79.56 g

Simple Turkey Tenderloin

Prep Time: 20 minutes| **Cook Time:** 30 minutes| **Serves:** 4

Olive oil
½ teaspoon paprika
½ teaspoon garlic powder
½ teaspoon salt
½ teaspoon freshly ground black pepper
Pinch cayenne pepper
675 g turkey breast tenderloin

1. Spray an air fryer basket lightly with olive oil. 2. In a small bowl, combine the paprika, garlic powder, salt, black pepper, and cayenne pepper. Rub the mixture all over the turkey. 3. Place the turkey in the air fryer basket and lightly spray with olive oil. 4. Air fry at 185 °C for 15 minutes. Flip the turkey over and lightly spray with olive oil. Air fry until the internal temperature reaches at least 75 °C for an additional 10 to 15 minutes. 5. Let the turkey rest for 10 minutes before slicing and serving.
Per Serving: Calories 264; Fat 4.79 g; Sodium 460 mg; Carbs 0.9 g; Fibre 0.3 g; Sugar 0.09 g; Protein 51.44 g

Turkey Burgers

Prep Time: 40 minutes| **Cook Time:** 20 minutes| **Serves:** 4

Olive oil
450 g lean turkey mince
30 g whole-wheat bread crumbs
60 ml hoisin sauce
2 tablespoons soy sauce
4 whole-wheat buns

1. Spray an air fryer basket lightly with olive oil. 2. In a large bowl, mix together the turkey, bread crumbs, hoisin sauce, and soy sauce. 3. Make 4 equal patties out from the mixture. Cover with plastic wrap and refrigerate the patties for 30 minutes. 4. Place the patties in the fryer basket in a single layer. Spray the patties lightly with olive oil. 5.Air fry at 185 °C for 10 minutes. Flip the patties over, lightly spray with olive oil, and cook until golden brown, an additional 5 to 10 minutes. 6. Add the patties onto buns and top with your choice of low-calorie burger toppings like sliced tomatoes, onions, and cabbage slaw.
Per Serving: Calories 340; Fat 13.65 g; Sodium 631 mg; Carbs 29.29 g; Fibre 3 g; Sugar 6.55 g; Protein 25.98 g

Apricot-Glazed Turkey Tenderloin

Prep Time: 20 minutes| **Cook Time:** 30 minutes| **Serves:** 4

Olive oil
80 g sugar-free apricot preserves
½ tablespoon spicy brown mustard
675 g turkey breast tenderloin
Salt
Freshly ground black pepper

1. Spray an air fryer basket lightly with olive oil. 2. Combine the apricot preserves and mustard in a small bowl to make a paste. 3. Season the turkey with salt and pepper. Spread the apricot paste all over the turkey. 4. Place the turkey in the air fryer basket and lightly spray with olive oil. 5. Air fry at 185 °C for 15 minutes. Flip the turkey over and lightly spray with olive oil. Air fry until the internal temperature reaches at least 75 °C, an additional 10 to 15 minutes. 6. Let the glazed turkey rest for 10 minutes before slicing and serving.
Per Serving: Calories 263; Fat 4.75 g; Sodium 235 mg; Carbs 0.54 g; Fibre 0.2 g; Sugar 0.02 g; Protein 51.45 g

Crispy Chicken Thighs and Carrots

Prep Time: 10 minutes| **Cook Time:** 22 minutes| **Serves:** 4

4 bone-in, skin-on chicken thighs
2 carrots, cut into 5 cm pieces
2 tablespoons extra-virgin olive oil
2 teaspoons poultry spice
1 teaspoon sea salt, divided
2 teaspoons chopped fresh rosemary leaves
Cooking oil spray
300 g cooked white rice

1. Brush the chicken thighs and carrots with olive oil. Sprinkle both with the poultry spice, salt, and rosemary. 2. Insert the crisper plate into the basket and the basket into the unit. Preheat the unit by selecting AIR FRY, setting the temperature to 205 °C, and setting the time to 3 minutes. Select START/STOP to begin. 3. Once the unit is preheated, spray the crisper plate with cooking oil. Place the carrots into the basket. Add the wire rack and arrange the chicken thighs on the rack. 4. Select AIR FRY, set the temperature to 205 °C, and set the time to 20 minutes. Select START/STOP to begin. 5. When the cooking is complete, check the chicken temperature. If a food thermometer inserted into the chicken registers 75 °C, remove the chicken from the air fryer, place it on a clean plate, and cover with aluminum foil to keep warm. Otherwise, resume cooking for 1 to 2 minutes longer. 6. The carrots can cook for 18 to 22 minutes and will be tender and caramelized; cooking time isn't as crucial for root vegetables. 7. Serve the chicken and carrots with the hot cooked rice.
Per Serving: Calories 595; Fat 36.5 g; Sodium 811 mg; Carbs 29.53 g; Fibre 1.1 g; Sugar 0.81 g; Protein 34.38 g

Spinach, Cheese and Chicken Meatballs

Prep Time: 30 minutes| **Cook Time:** 18 minutes| **Serves:** 6

Olive oil
100 g fresh spinach, chopped
½ teaspoon salt, plus more as needed
55 g panko bread crumbs
¼ teaspoon freshly ground black pepper
¼ teaspoon garlic powder
1 egg, beaten
450 g chicken mince
80 g crumbled feta cheese

1. Spray a large skillet lightly with olive oil. Add the spinach, season lightly with salt, and cook over medium heat until the spinach has wilted, for 2 to 3 minutes. Set aside. 2. In a large bowl, mix together the panko bread crumbs, ½ teaspoon of salt, black pepper, and garlic powder. Add the egg, chicken, spinach, and feta cheese and stir to gently combine. 3. Using a heaping tablespoon, form 24 meatballs. 4. Lightly spray a fryer basket with olive oil. 5. Then place the meatballs in the air fryer basket in a single layer. Spray the meatballs lightly with olive oil. Cook them in batches as needed. 6. Air fry at 175 °C for 7 minutes. Turn the meatballs over and cook until golden brown, an additional 5 to 8 minutes.
Per Serving: Calories 193; Fat 9.59 g; Sodium 340 mg; Carbs 9.55 g; Fibre 0.7 g; Sugar 0.48 g; Protein 17.22 g

Breaded Chicken Strips

Prep Time: 15 minutes| **Cook Time:** 20 minutes| **Serves:** 4

1 tablespoon of olive oil, plus more for spraying
450 g boneless, skinless chicken tenderloins
1 teaspoon salt
½ teaspoon freshly ground black pepper
½ teaspoon paprika
½ teaspoon garlic powder
55 g seasoned bread crumbs
1 teaspoon dried parsley

1. Spray an air fryer basket lightly with olive oil. 2. Toss the chicken with the salt, black pepper, paprika, and garlic powder in a medium bowl until evenly coated. 3. Add the olive oil and toss to coat the chicken evenly. 4. In a separate, shallow bowl, mix together the bread crumbs and parsley. 5. Coat each piece of chicken evenly in the bread crumb mixture. 6. Transfer the chicken tenderloins to the air fryer basket in a single layer and spray it lightly with olive oil. Cook them in batches as needed. 7. Air fry at 185 °C for 10 minutes. Flip the chicken over, lightly spray with olive oil, and cook until golden brown, an additional 8 to 10 minutes.
Per Serving: Calories 216; Fat 7.31 g; Sodium 868 mg; Carbs 10.94 g; Fibre 1 g; Sugar 0.91 g; Protein 25.32 g

Mexican Sheet Pan Chicken Supper

Prep Time: 10 minutes| **Cook Time:** 15 minutes| **Serves:** 4

450 g boneless, skinless chicken tenderloins, cut into strips
3 peppers, any colour, cut into chunks
1 onion, cut into chunks
1 tablespoon olive oil, plus more for spraying
1 tablespoon fajita seasoning mix

1. In a large bowl, mix together the chicken, peppers, onion, 1 tablespoon of olive oil, and fajita seasoning mix until completely coated. 2. Spray an air fryer basket lightly with olive oil. 3. Place the chicken and vegetables in the fryer basket and lightly spray with olive oil. 4. Air fry at 185 °C for 7 minutes. Shake the basket and cook until the chicken is cooked through and the veggies are starting to char, an additional 5 to 8 minutes.
Per Serving: Calories 203; Fat 6.57 g; Sodium 249 mg; Carbs 10.69 g; Fibre 1.5 g; Sugar 6.11 g; Protein 24.49 g

Marinara Chicken with Cheeses

Prep Time: 10 minutes| **Cook Time:** 20 minutes| **Serves:** 4

2 (100 g) boneless, skinless chicken breasts
2 egg whites, beaten
110 g Italian bread crumbs
50 g grated Parmesan cheese
2 teaspoons Italian seasoning
Salt
Freshly ground black pepper
Cooking oil spray
200 g marinara sauce
55 g shredded mozzarella cheese

1. Cut the boneless and skinless chicken breasts in half horizontally to create 4 thin cutlets on a cutting board with a knife blade parallel. On a solid surface, pound the cutlets to flatten them with your hands, a rolling pin, a kitchen mallet, or a meat hammer. 2. Pour the egg whites into a bowl large enough to dip the chicken. 3. In another bowl large enough to dip a chicken cutlet in, stir together the bread crumbs, Parmesan cheese, and Italian seasoning, and season with salt and pepper. 4. Dip each cutlet into the egg whites and into the breadcrumb mixture to coat. 5. Insert the crisper plate into the basket and the basket into the unit. Preheat the unit by selecting AIR FRY, setting the temperature to 190 °C, and setting the time to 3 minutes. Select START/STOP to begin. 6. Once the unit is preheated, spray the crisper plate with cooking oil. Working in batches, place 2 chicken cutlets into the basket. Spray the chicken with cooking oil. 7. Select AIR FRY, set the temperature to 190 °C, and set the time to 7 minutes. Select START/STOP to begin. 8. When the cooking is complete, repeat steps 6 and 7 with the remaining cutlets. 9. Top the chicken cutlets with the marinara sauce and shredded mozzarella cheese. If the chicken will fit into the basket without stacking, you can prepare all 4 at once. Otherwise, do these 2 cutlets at a time. 10. Select AIR FRY, set the temperature to 190 °C, and set the time to 3 minutes. Select START/STOP to begin. 11. The cooking is complete when the cheese is melted and the chicken reaches an internal temperature of 75 °C. Cool for 5 minutes before serving.
Per Serving: Calories 192; Fat 8.26 g; Sodium 574 mg; Carbs 11.41 g; Fibre 1.6 g; Sugar 3.64 g; Protein 17.26 g

Sweet and Spicy General Tso's Chicken

Prep Time: 10 minutes| **Cook Time:** 14 minutes| **Serves:** 4

1 tablespoon sesame oil
1 teaspoon minced garlic
½ teaspoon ground ginger
240 ml chicken stock
4 tablespoons soy sauce, divided
½ teaspoon sriracha, plus more for serving
2 tablespoons hoisin sauce
4 tablespoons cornflour, divided
4 boneless, skinless chicken breasts, cut into 2.5 cm pieces
Olive oil spray
2 medium spring onions, sliced, green parts only
Sesame seeds, for garnish

1. Set a suitable saucepan over low heat, combine the sesame oil, garlic, and ginger and cook for 1 minute. 2. Add the chicken stock, 2 tablespoons of soy sauce, the sriracha, and hoisin sauce. Whisk to combine. 3. Whisk in 2 tablespoons of cornflour and continue cooking over low heat until the sauce starts to thicken, about 5 minutes. Remove the pan from heat, cover, and then set aside. 4. Insert the crisper plate into the basket and the basket into the unit. Preheat the unit by selecting BAKE, setting the temperature 205 °C, and setting the time to 3 minutes. Select START/STOP to begin. 5. Toss together the chicken, remaining 2 tablespoons of soy sauce, and remaining 2 tablespoons of cornflour in a medium bowl. 6. Once the unit is preheated, spray the crisper plate with olive oil. Place the chicken into the basket and spray it with olive oil. 7. Select BAKE, set the temperature to 205 °C, and set the time to 9 minutes. Select START/STOP to begin. 8. After 5 minutes, remove the basket, shake, and spray the chicken with more olive oil. Reinsert the basket to resume cooking. 9. When the cooking is up, a food thermometer inserted into the chicken should register at least 75 °C. Transfer the chicken breasts to a large bowl and toss it with the sauce. Garnish with the spring onions and sesame seeds and serve.
Per Serving: Calories 308; Fat 11.62 g; Sodium 680 mg; Carbs 16.06 g; Fibre 0.9 g; Sugar 5.72 g; Protein 32.7 g

Spicy Chicken and Potatoes

Prep Time: 5 minutes| **Cook Time:** 25 minutes| **Serves:** 4

4 bone-in, skin-on chicken thighs
½ teaspoon salt or ¼ teaspoon fine salt
2 tablespoons melted unsalted butter
2 teaspoons Worcestershire sauce
2 teaspoons curry powder
1 teaspoon dried oregano leaves
½ teaspoon dry mustard
½ teaspoon granulated garlic
¼ teaspoon paprika
¼ teaspoon hot pepper sauce, such as Tabasco
Cooking oil spray
4 medium Yukon gold potatoes, chopped
1 tablespoon extra-virgin olive oil

1. Sprinkle salt over both sides of the chicken thighs. 2. Stir together the melted butter, Worcestershire sauce, curry powder, oregano, dry mustard, granulated garlic, paprika, and your favored hot pepper sauce in a medium bowl. Add the thighs to the sauce and stir to coat. 3. Insert the crisper plate into the basket and the basket into the unit. Preheat the unit by selecting AIR FRY, setting the temperature to 205 °C, and setting the time to 3 minutes. Select START/STOP to begin. 4. Once the unit is preheated, spray the crisper plate with cooking oil. In the basket, combine the potatoes and olive oil and toss to coat. 5. Add the wire rack to the air fryer and place the chicken thighs on top. 6. Select AIR FRY, set the temperature setting to 205 °C, and set the time to 25 minutes. Select START/STOP to begin. 7. After 19 minutes check the chicken thighs. If a food thermometer inserted into the chicken registers 75 °C, transfer them to a clean plate, and then cover it with aluminum foil to keep warm. If they aren't cooked to 75 °C, resume cooking for another 1 to 2 minutes until they are done. Remove them from the air fryer along with the rack. 8. Remove the basket and shake it to distribute the potatoes. Reinsert the basket to resume cooking for 3 to 6 minutes, or until the potatoes are crisp and golden brown. 9. When the cooking is complete, serve the chicken with the potatoes.
Per Serving: Calories 656; Fat 38.92 g; Sodium 536 mg; Carbs 39.22 g; Fibre 5.4 g; Sugar 2.02 g; Protein 36.66 g

Buttermilk Fried Chicken

Prep Time: 7 minutes| **Cook Time:** 20 to 25 minutes| **Serves:** 4

125 g plain flour
2 teaspoons paprika
Pinch salt
Freshly ground black pepper
80 ml buttermilk
2 eggs
2 tablespoons extra-virgin olive oil
160 g bread crumbs
6 chicken pieces, drumsticks, breasts, and thigh
Cooking oil spray

1. In a shallow bowl, stir together the flour, paprika, salt, and pepper. 2. In another bowl, beat the buttermilk and eggs until smooth. 3. In a third bowl, stir together the olive oil and bread crumbs until mixed. 4. Dredge the chicken in the flour, dip in the eggs to coat, and finally press into the bread crumbs, patting the crumbs firmly onto the chicken skin. 5. Insert the crisper plate into the basket and the basket into the unit. Preheat the unit by selecting AIR FRY, setting the temperature to 190 °C, and setting the time to 3 minutes. Select START/STOP to begin. 6. Once the unit is preheated, spray the crisper plate with cooking oil. Place the chicken into the basket. 7. Select AIR FRY, set the temperature to 190 °C, and set the time to 25 minutes. Select START/STOP to begin. 8. After 10 minutes, flip the chicken. Resume cooking. After 10 minutes more, check the chicken. If a food thermometer inserted into the chicken registers 75 °C and the chicken is brown and crisp, it is done. Otherwise, resume cooking for up to 5 minutes longer. 9. When the cooking is complete, let cool for 5 minutes, then serve.
Per Serving: Calories 679; Fat 31.45 g; Sodium 399 mg; Carbs 32.45 g; Fibre 1.7 g; Sugar 2 g; Protein 62.49 g

Ranch Chicken Wings

Prep Time: 10 minutes, plus 30 minutes to marinate| **Cook Time:** 40 minutes| **Serves:** 4

2 tablespoons water
2 tablespoons hot pepper sauce
2 tablespoons unsalted butter, melted
2 tablespoons apple cider vinegar
1 (25 g) envelope ranch salad dressing mix
1 teaspoon paprika
1.8 kg chicken wings, tips removed
Cooking oil spray

1. In a large bowl, whisk the water, hot pepper sauce, melted butter, vinegar, salad dressing mix, and paprika until combined. 2. Add the wings and toss to coat. Then cover the bowl and marinate the wings in the refrigerator for 4 to 24 hours for best results. However, you can just let the wings stand for 30 minutes in the refrigerator. 3. Insert the crisper plate into the air fryer basket and the air fryer basket into the unit. Preheat the air fryer by selecting AIR FRY, setting the temperature to 205 °C, and setting the timer to 3 minutes. 4. Once the unit is preheated, spray the crisper plate with cooking oil. Working in batches, put half the wings into the basket; it is okay to stack them. Refrigerate the remaining wings. 5. Select AIR FRY, set the temperature to 205 °C, and set the time to 20 minutes. Select START/STOP to begin. 6. Remove and shake the air fryer basket every 5 minutes, three more times, until the chicken is browned and glazed and a food thermometer inserted into the wings registers 75 °C. 7. Repeat the cooking steps with the remaining wings. 8. When the cooking is complete, serve warm.

Per Serving: Calories 660; Fat 24.5 g; Sodium 440 mg; Carbs 2.94 g; Fibre 0.5 g; Sugar 1.59 g; Protein 100.52 g

Korean Chicken Wings

Prep Time: 10 minutes| **Cook Time:** 25 minutes per batch | **Serves:** 4

65 g gochujang, or red pepper paste
55 g mayonnaise
2 tablespoons honey
1 tablespoon sesame oil
2 teaspoons minced garlic
1 tablespoon sugar
2 teaspoons ground ginger
1.3 kg whole chicken wings
Olive oil spray
1 teaspoon salt
½ teaspoon freshly ground black pepper

1. In a large bowl, whisk the gochujang, mayonnaise, honey, sesame oil, garlic, sugar, and ginger. Set aside. 2. Insert the crisper plate into the basket and the basket into the unit. Preheat the unit by selecting AIR FRY, setting the temperature to 205 °C, and setting the time to 3 minutes. Select START/STOP to begin. 3. To prepare the chicken wings, cut the wings in half. The meatier part is the drumette. Cut off and discard the wing tip from the flat part (or save the wing tips in the freezer to make chicken stock). 4. Once the unit is preheated, spray the crisper plate with olive oil. Working in batches, place half the chicken wings into the basket, spray them with olive oil, and sprinkle with the salt and pepper. 5. Select AIR FRY, set the temperature to 205 °C, and set the time to 20 minutes. Select START/STOP to begin. 6. After 10 minutes, remove the basket, flip the wings, and spray them with more olive oil. Reinsert the basket to resume cooking. 7. Cook the wings to an internal temperature of 75 °C, then transfer them to the bowl with the prepared sauce and toss to coat. 8. Repeat steps 4, 5, 6, and 7 for the remaining chicken wings. 9. Return the coated wings to the basket and air fry for 4 to 6 minutes more until the sauce has glazed the wings and the chicken is crisp. After 3 minutes, check the wings to make sure they aren't burning. Serve hot.

Per Serving: Calories 563; Fat 21.39 g; Sodium 974 mg; Carbs 12.48 g; Fibre 0.4 g; Sugar 10.89 g; Protein 75.89 g

Buffalo Crumb-Crusted Chicken Strips

Prep Time: 15 minutes| **Cook Time:** 13 to 17 minutes per batch| **Serves:** 4

95 g flour
2 eggs
2 tablespoons water
110 g seasoned panko bread crumbs
2 teaspoons granulated garlic
1 teaspoon salt
1 teaspoon freshly ground black pepper
16 chicken breast strips, or 3 large boneless, skinless chicken breasts, cut into 2.5 cm strips
Olive oil spray
60 ml Buffalo sauce, plus more as needed

1. Put the plain flour in a small bowl. 2. In another small bowl, whisk the eggs and the water. 3. In a third bowl, stir the panko, granulated garlic, salt, and pepper together. 4. Then dip each chicken strip in the flour, in the egg, and in the panko mixture to coat. Press the crumbs onto the chicken with your fingers. 5. Insert the crisper plate into the basket and the basket into the unit. Preheat the unit by selecting AIR FRY, setting the temperature to 190 °C, and setting the time to 3 minutes. Select START/STOP to begin. 6. Once the unit is preheated, place a parchment paper liner into the basket. Place the chicken strips evenly into the basket, working in batches as needed. Do not stack unless using a wire rack for the second layer. Spray the chicken with olive oil. 7. Select AIR FRY, set the temperature to 190 °C, and set the time to 17 minutes. Select START/STOP to begin. 8. After 10 or 12 minutes, remove the basket, flip the chicken, and spray again with olive oil. Reinsert the basket to resume cooking. 9. When the cooking is up, the chicken should be golden brown and crispy and a food thermometer inserted into the chicken should reach 75 °C. 10. Repeat steps 6, 7, and 8 with any remaining chicken. 11. Transfer the chicken to a large bowl. Drizzle the Buffalo sauce over the top of the cooked chicken, toss to coat, and serve.
Per Serving: Calories 409; Fat 15.95 g; Sodium 922 mg; Carbs 30.5 g; Fibre 1.2 g; Sugar 6.6 g; Protein 33.46 g

Homemade Chicken Satay

Prep Time: 12 minutes| **Cook Time:** 12 to 18 minutes| **Serves:** 4

50 g crunchy peanut butter
80 ml chicken stock
3 tablespoons low-sodium soy sauce
2 tablespoons freshly squeezed lemon juice
2 garlic cloves, minced
2 tablespoons extra-virgin olive oil
1 teaspoon curry powder
455 g chicken tenders
Cooking oil spray

1. Whisk the peanut butter, chicken stock, soy sauce, lemon juice, garlic, olive oil, and curry powder in a medium bowl until smooth. 2. Place 2 tablespoons of this mixture into a small bowl. Transfer the remaining sauce to a serving bowl and set aside. 3. Add the chicken tenders to the bowl with the 2 tablespoons of sauce and stir to coat. Let stand for a few minutes to marinate. 4. Insert the crisper plate into the basket and the basket into the unit. Preheat the unit by selecting AIR FRY, setting the temperature to 200 °C, and setting the time to 3 minutes. Select START/STOP to begin. 5. Run a 15 cm bamboo skewer lengthwise through each chicken tender. 6. Once the unit is preheated, spray the crisper plate with cooking oil. Working in batches, place half the chicken skewers into the basket in a single layer without overlapping. 7. Select AIR FRY, set the temperature to 200 °C, and set the time to 9 minutes. Select START/STOP to begin. 8. After 6 minutes, check the chicken. If a food thermometer inserted into the chicken registers 75 °C, it is done. If not, resume cooking. 9. Repeat the 6, 7, and 8 steps with the remaining chicken. 10. When the cooking is complete, serve the chicken with the reserved sauce.
Per Serving: Calories 363; Fat 19.6 g; Sodium 799 mg; Carbs 14.82 g; Fibre 2.3 g; Sugar 3.7 g; Protein 33.69 g

Crispy Mayo Chicken Tenders

Prep Time: 10 minutes| **Cook Time:** 15 minutes| **Serves:** 4

110 g panko bread crumbs
1 tablespoon paprika
½ teaspoon salt
¼ teaspoon freshly ground black pepper
16 chicken tenders
110 g mayonnaise
Olive oil spray

1. Stir together the panko, paprika, salt, and pepper in a medium bowl. 2. Toss together the chicken tenders and mayonnaise in a large bowl to coat. Transfer the mayo-coated chicken pieces to the bowl of seasoned panko and dredge to coat thoroughly. Press with your fingers until firmly coated. 3. Insert the crisper plate into the basket and the basket into the unit. Preheat the unit by selecting AIR FRY, setting the temperature to 175 °C, and setting the time to 3 minutes. Select START/STOP to begin. 4. Once the unit is preheated, place a parchment paper liner into the basket. Place the chicken into the basket and spray it with olive oil. 5. Select AIR FRY, set the temperature to 175 °C, and set the time to 15 minutes. Select START/STOP to begin. 6. When the cooking is complete, the tenders will be golden brown and a food thermometer inserted into the chicken should register 75 °C. For more even browning, remove the basket halfway through cooking and flip the tenders. Give them an extra spray of olive oil and reinsert the basket to resume cooking. This ensures they are crispy and brown all over. 7. When the cooking is complete, serve.
Per Serving: Calories 407; Fat 16.91 g; Sodium 849 mg; Carbs 21.37 g; Fibre 2.2 g; Sugar 2.11 g; Protein 40.23 g

Chicken Cordon Bleu

Prep Time: 15 minutes| **Cook Time:** 15 minutes| **Serves:** 4

4 chicken breast filets
70 g chopped ham
70 g grated Swiss cheese, or Gruyère cheese
30 g plain flour
Pinch salt
Freshly ground black pepper
½ teaspoon dried marjoram
1 egg
110 g panko bread crumbs
Olive oil spray

1. Place the chicken breast filets on a work surface and then gently press the chicken to make them thinner with the palm of your hand but to watch out not to tear them. 2. Combine the ham and cheese in a small bowl. Divide the mixture among the chicken filets. Then wrap the chicken rolls, using toothpicks to hold the chicken together. 3. Stir together the flour, salt, pepper, and marjoram in a shallow bowl. 4. In another bowl, beat the egg. 5. Spread the panko on a plate. 6. Dip the chicken in the flour mixture, in the egg, and in the panko to coat thoroughly. Press the panko crumbs into the chicken so they stick well. 7. Insert the crisper plate into the basket and the basket into the unit. Preheat the unit by selecting BAKE, setting the temperature to 190 °C, and setting the time to 3 minutes. Select START/STOP to begin. 8. Once the unit is preheated, spray the crisper plate with olive oil. Place the chicken into the basket and spray it with olive oil. 9. Select BAKE, set the temperature to 190 °C, and set the time to 15 minutes. Select START/STOP to begin. 10. When the cooking is up, the chicken should be cooked through and a food thermometer inserted into the chicken should register 75 °C. Carefully remove the toothpicks and serve.
Per Serving: Calories 464; Fat 20.54 g; Sodium 459 mg; Carbs 26.22 g; Fibre 1.5 g; Sugar 1.97 g; Protein 40.79 g

Pineapple Chicken Kebabs

Prep Time: 15 minutes, plus 1 to 2 hours to marinate| **Cook Time:** 20 minutes| **Serves:** 6

Olive oil
3 tablespoons soy sauce
1 (375 g) can pineapple chunks, 2 tablespoons of the juice reserved
1 tablespoon sesame oil
¼ teaspoon ground ginger
¼ teaspoon garlic powder
775 g boneless, skinless chicken breasts, cut into 2.5 cm chunks
2 large peppers

1. Spray an air fryer basket lightly with olive oil. Cut the peppers into 2.5 cm chunks. 2.Mix together the soy sauce, the reserved pineapple juice, sesame oil, ginger, and garlic powder in a large bowl. Add the chicken, peppers, and pineapple chunks and toss to coat. 3.Cover the bowl and then refrigerate it for at least 1 hour and up to 2 hours. 4.If using wooden skewers, soak the skewers in water for at least 30 minutes. 5.Thread the chicken, peppers, and pineapple onto the skewers, alternating with chicken, vegetable, and fruit. Place the skewers in the air fryer basket in a single layer. Lightly spray the skewers with olive oil. Cook the kebabs in batches as needed. 6.Air fry at 175 °C for 10 minutes. Turn the skewers over, lightly spray with olive oil, and cook until the chicken is nicely browned and the veggies are starting to char on the edges, for an additional 5 to 10 minutes.
Per Serving: Calories 235; Fat 7.52 g; Sodium 173 mg; Carbs 14.69 g; Fibre 1 g; Sugar 12.55 g; Protein 26.71 g

Savory Sesame Chicken Tenders

Prep Time: 5 minutes, plus 2 hours to marinate| **Cook Time:** 15 minutes| **Serves:** 4

Olive oil
60 ml soy sauce
2 tablespoons white vinegar
1 tablespoon honey
1 tablespoon toasted sesame oil
1 tablespoon lime juice
1 teaspoon ground ginger
450 g boneless skinless, chicken tenderloins
2 teaspoon toasted sesame seeds

1. Spray an air fryer basket lightly with olive oil. 2. In a large zip-top plastic bag, combine the soy sauce, white vinegar, honey, sesame oil, lime juice, and ginger to make a marinade. 3. Add the chicken tenderloins to the bag, seal, and marinate the chicken in the refrigerator for at least 2 hours or overnight. 4. Thread 1 chicken tenderloin onto each skewer. Sprinkle with sesame seeds. Reserve the marinade. (For wooden skewers, soak them in water for at least 30 minutes.) 5. Place the skewers in the fryer basket in a single layer. You may need to cook the chicken in batches. 6.Air fry at 190 °C for 6 minutes. Flip the chicken over, baste with more marinade, and cook until crispy, an additional 5 to 8 minutes.
Per Serving: Calories 237; Fat 9.91 g; Sodium 307 mg; Carbs 9.34 g; Fibre 0.6 g; Sugar 7.5 g; Protein 26.61 g

Teriyaki Chicken and Broccoli Bowls

Prep Time: 5 minutes, plus up to 30 minutes to marinate| **Cook Time:** 15 minutes| **Serves:** 4

Olive oil
80 ml soy sauce
110 g honey
3 tablespoons white vinegar
1½ teaspoons dried thyme
1½ teaspoons paprika
1 teaspoon ground black pepper
½ teaspoon cayenne pepper
½ teaspoon ground allspice
450 g boneless, skinless chicken tenderloins
300 g cooked brown rice
180 g steamed broccoli florets

1. Spray an air fryer basket lightly with olive oil. 2. Mix together the soy sauce, honey, white vinegar, thyme, paprika, black pepper, cayenne pepper, and allspice in a large bowl to make a marinade. 3. Add the tenderloins to the marinade and stir to coat. Cover and refrigerate for 30 minutes. 4. Place the chicken in the fryer basket in a single layer. Cook the chicken in batches as needed. Reserve the marinade. 5. Air fry at 190 °C for 6 minutes. Turn the chicken over and brush with some of the remaining marinade. Cook until chicken reaches an internal temperature of at least 75 °C, an additional 5 to 7 minutes. 6. To assemble the bowls, place 80 g of brown rice, 45 g of steamed broccoli, and 2 chicken tenderloins into each bowl and serve.
Per Serving: Calories 402; Fat 7.89 g; Sodium 386 mg; Carbs 53.19 g; Fibre 3.4 g; Sugar 27.61 g; Protein 29.91 g

Chicken Wraps

Prep Time: 1 hour 10 minutes| **Cook Time:** 15 minutes| **Serves:** 4

450 g boneless, skinless chicken tenderloins
135 g jerk marinade
Olive oil
4 large low-carb tortillas
130 g julienned carrots
120 g peeled cucumber ribbons
35 g shredded lettuce
165 g mango or pineapple chunks

1. In a medium bowl, coat the chicken with the jerk marinade, cover, and refrigerate for 1 hour. 2. Spray a fryer basket lightly with olive oil. 3. Place the chicken in the fryer basket in a single layer and spray lightly with olive oil. You may need to cook the chicken in batches. Reserve any leftover marinade. 4. Air fry at 190 °C for 8 minutes. Turn the chicken over and brush with some of the remaining marinade. Cook the chicken until the internal   chicken part reaches at least 75 °C, an additional 5 to 7 minutes. 5. To assemble the wraps, fill each tortilla with 35 g carrots, 30 g cucumber ribbons, 10 g lettuce, and 40 g mango. Place one quarter of the chicken tenderloins on top and roll up the tortilla. These are great served warm or cold.
Per Serving: Calories 425; Fat 16.73 g; Sodium 1072 mg; Carbs 38.83 g; Fibre 4.6 g; Sugar 20.02 g; Protein 30.17 g

Balsamic Chicken and Veggies

Prep Time: 10 minutes| **Cook Time:** 30 minutes| **Serves:** 4

180 ml balsamic vinaigrette dressing, divided
450 g boneless, skinless chicken tenderloins
Olive oil
450 g fresh green beans, trimmed
340 g grape tomatoes

1. Place 120 ml of the balsamic vinaigrette dressing and the chicken in a large zip-top plastic bag, seal, and refrigerate for at least 1 hour or up to overnight. 2. Mix together the green beans, tomatoes, and the remaining 60 ml of balsamic vinaigrette dressing in a large bowl until well coated. 3. Spray the fryer basket lightly with olive oil. Place the vegetables in the fryer basket. Reserve any remaining vinaigrette. 4. Air fry at 185 °C to 205 °C for 8 minutes. Shake the air fryer basket and continue to cook until the beans are crisp but tender, and the tomatoes are soft and slightly charred, an additional 5 to 7 minutes. 5. Wipe the fryer basket with a paper towel and spray lightly with olive oil. 6. Place the chicken in the fryer basket in a single layer. Cook them in batches as needed. 7. Air fry at 185 °C to 205 °C for 7 minutes. Flip the chicken over, baste with some of the remaining vinaigrette, and cook until the chicken reaches an internal temperature of 75 °C, an additional 5 to 8 minutes. 8. Serve the chicken and veggies together.
Per Serving: Calories 188; Fat 4.62 g; Sodium 97 mg; Carbs 11.66 g; Fibre 4.6 g; Sugar 5.66 g; Protein 26.02 g

Italian Roasted Whole Chicken

Prep Time: 15 minutes| **Cook Time:** 1 hour| **Serves:** 6

Olive oil
1 teaspoon salt
1 teaspoon Italian seasoning
½ teaspoon freshly ground black pepper
½ teaspoon paprika
½ teaspoon garlic powder
½ teaspoon onion powder
2 tablespoons olive oil
1 (1.8) fryer chicken

1. Spray an air fryer basket lightly with olive oil. 2. Mix together the salt, Italian seasoning, black pepper, paprika, garlic powder, and onion powder in a small bowl. 3. Remove any giblets from the chicken. Then use paper towels to pat the fryer chicken dry, including the cavity. 4. Brush the chicken all over with the olive oil and rub it with the seasoning mixture. 5. Truss the chicken or tie the legs with butcher's twine. This will make it easier to flip the chicken during cooking. 6. Place the chicken in the fryer basket, breast side down. Air fry for 30 minutes. Flip the chicken over and baste it with any drippings collected in the bottom drawer of the air fryer. Lightly spray the chicken with olive oil. 7. Air fry at 180 °C for 20 minutes. Flip the chicken over one last time and cook until a thermometer inserted into the thickest part of the thigh reaches at least 75 °C and it's crispy and golden, 10 more minutes. Continue to cook, checking every 5 minutes until the chicken reaches the correct internal temperature. 8. Let the roasted chicken stand for 10 minutes before carving.
Per Serving: Calories 410; Fat 14.6 g; Sodium 656 mg; Carbs 0.87 g; Fibre 0.2 g; Sugar 0.09 g; Protein 64.82 g

Turkey-bread Meatballs

Prep Time: 15 minutes| **Cook Time:** 15 minutes| **Serves:** 6

Olive oil
450 g lean turkey mince
55 g panko bread crumbs
1 egg, beaten
1 tablespoon soy sauce
60 ml plus 1 tablespoon hoisin sauce, divided
2 teaspoons minced garlic
⅛ teaspoon salt
⅛ teaspoon freshly ground black pepper
1 teaspoon sriracha

1. Spray an air fryer basket lightly with olive oil. 2. Mix together the turkey, panko bread crumbs, egg, soy sauce, 1 tablespoon of hoisin sauce, garlic, salt, and black pepper in a large bowl. 3. Using a tablespoon, form 24 meatballs. 4. Combine the remaining 60 ml of hoisin sauce and sriracha in a small bowl to make a glaze and set aside. 5. Place the meatballs in the fryer basket in a single layer. You may need to cook them in batches. 6. Air fry at 175 °C for 8 minutes. Generously brush the glaze over the meatballs and cook until cooked through, an additional 4 to 7 minutes.
Per Serving: Calories 184; Fat 8.45 g; Sodium 238 mg; Carbs 10.12 g; Fibre 0.6 g; Sugar 1.05 g; Protein 16.88 g

Cheddar Stuffed Peppers

Prep Time: 20 minutes| **Cook Time:** 15 minutes| **Serves:** 4

225 g lean turkey mince
4 medium peppers
1 (375 g) can black beans, drained and rinsed
100 g shredded reduced-fat Cheddar cheese
200 g cooked long-grain brown rice
250 g mild salsa
1¼ teaspoons chili powder
1 teaspoon salt
½ teaspoon ground cumin
½ teaspoon freshly ground black pepper
Olive oil
Chopped fresh coriander, for garnish

1. In a large skillet over medium-high heat, cook the turkey, breaking it up with a spoon, until browned, about 5 minutes. Drain off any excess fat. 2. Cut about 1 cm off the tops of the peppers and then cut in half lengthwise. Remove and discard the seeds and set the peppers aside. 3. In a large bowl, combine the browned turkey, black beans, Cheddar cheese, rice, salsa, chili powder, salt, cumin, and black pepper. Spoon the mixture into the peppers. 4. Lightly spray an air fryer basket with olive oil. 5. Place the stuffed peppers in the air fryer basket. Air fry at 180 °C until heated throughout, 10 to 15 minutes. Garnish with coriander and serve.
Per Serving: Calories 263; Fat 9.33 g; Sodium 1399 mg; Carbs 24.29 g; Fibre 4.5 g; Sugar 5.83 g; Protein 22.82 g

Beef Taco Rolls

Prep Time: 20 minutes| **Cook Time:** 10 minutes| **Serves:** 4

225 g lean beef mince
80 ml water
1 tablespoon chili powder
2 teaspoons cumin
½ teaspoon garlic powder
¼ teaspoon dried oregano
60 g canned diced tomatoes and chiles, drained
2 tablespoons chopped coriander
170 g shredded mozzarella cheese
50 g blanched finely ground almond flour
50 g full-fat cream cheese
1 large egg

1. Brown the beef mince for about 7–10 minutes in a medium frying pan over medium heat. Drain the meat when it is fully cooked. 2. Add water to the frying pan and stir in chili powder, cumin, garlic powder, oregano, and tomatoes with chiles. Add coriander. 3. Bring them together to a boil, then reduce heat to simmer for 3 minutes. 4. Place mozzarella, almond flour, cream cheese, and the egg in a large microwave-safe bowl. Microwave for 1 minute. Stir the mixture quickly until smooth ball of dough forms. 5. Cut a piece of parchment for your work surface. Press the dough into a large rectangle on the parchment, wetting your hands to prevent the dough from sticking as necessary. Cut the dough into eight rectangles. 6. Place a few spoons of the meat mixture on each rectangle. Fold the short ends of each roll toward the centre and roll the length as you would to make a burrito. 7. Cut a suitable piece of parchment to fit your air fryer basket. Place taco rolls onto the parchment and place into the air fryer basket, adjust the temperature setting to 180 °C and set the timer for 10 minutes. Flip halfway through cooking. 8. Cool for 10 minutes before serving.
Per Serving: Calories 374; Fat 23g; Sodium 492mg; Carbs 8g; Fibre 3.5g; Sugar 2.3g; Protein 35g

Beef Empanadas with Cheeses

Prep Time: 15 minutes| **Cook Time:** 25 minutes| **Serves:** 15

Cooking oil
2 garlic cloves, chopped
50 g chopped green pepper
⅓ medium onion, chopped
200 g lean beef mince
1 teaspoon burger seasoning
Salt
Pepper
15 empanada wrappers
115 g shredded mozzarella cheese
100 g shredded Pepper Jack cheese
1 tablespoon butter

1. Spray a frying pan with cooking oil and turn medium-high heat on. Add garlic, green pepper, and onion. Cook for about 2 minutes until fragrant. 2. Add the beef mince to the frying pan. Season the beef with the hamburger seasoning, salt, and pepper. Use a spatula to break up the beef into small pieces. Cook the beef until browned. Drain any excess fat. 3. Lay the empanada wrappers on a flat surface. 4. Dip a basting brush in water. Glaze each empanada wrapper with a wet brush along the edges to soften the crust and make it easier to roll.) 5. Scoop 2 to 3 tablespoons of beef mixture onto each empanada wrapper. Sprinkle the mozzarella and Pepper Jack cheeses over the beef mixture. 6. Close the empanadas by folding the empanada in half. Press along and seal the edges with the back of a fork. 7. Place 7 or 8 of the empanadas in the air fryer. Spray each with cooking oil. Cook at 205 °C for 8 minutes. 8. Open the air fryer and flip the empanadas. Cook for an additional 4 minutes. 9. Remove the cooked empanadas from the air fryer, then repeat the empanada-preparing steps for the remaining empanadas. 10. For added flavour, melt the butter in the microwave for 20 seconds. Use a cooking brush to spread the melted butter over the top of each. 11. Cool before serving.
Per Serving: Calories 176; Fat 5.3g; Sodium 314mg; Carbs 19.8g; Fibre 0.8g; Sugar 0.5g; Protein 11.5g

Mouth-watering Pork Chop Salad

Prep Time: 15 minutes| **Cook Time:** 8 minutes| **Serves:** 2

1 tablespoon coconut oil
2 (100 g) pork chops, chopped into 2.5 cm cubes
2 teaspoons chili powder
1 teaspoon paprika
½ teaspoon garlic powder
¼ teaspoon onion powder
315 g chopped romaine
1 medium Roma tomato, diced
50 g shredded Monterey jack cheese
1 medium avocado, peeled, pitted, and diced
60 g full-fat ranch dressing
1 tablespoon chopped coriander

1. Chop the pork into 2.5 cm cubes. Drizzle coconut oil over the cubes in a large bowl. Sprinkle them with chili powder, paprika, garlic powder, and onion powder. 2. Place them into your air fryer basket, adjust the temperature setting to 205 °C and then set the timer for 8 minutes. The pork cubes will be golden and crispy when fully cooked. 3. Place romaine, tomato, and crispy pork in a large bowl. Top with shredded cheese and avocado. Pour ranch dressing around bowl and toss the salad to evenly coat. 5. Top with coriander. 6. Serve immediately.
Per Serving: Calories 576; Fat 37g; Sodium 354mg; Carbs 10.7g; Fibre 9g; Sugar 4.3g; Protein 34g

BBQ Meatballs

Prep Time: 10 minutes| **Cook Time:** 14 minutes| **Serves:** 4

455 g beef mince
110 g Italian sausage meat
1 large egg
¼ teaspoon onion powder
½ teaspoon garlic powder
1 teaspoon dried parsley
4 slices bacon, cooked and chopped
40 g chopped white onion
25 g chopped pickled jalapeños
125 g low-carb, sugar-free barbecue sauce

1. Mix beef mince, sausage, and egg in a large bowl until fully combined. Mix in all remaining ingredients except barbecue sauce. 2. Form into eight meatballs. Place meatballs into the air fryer basket, adjust the temperature to 205 °C and set the timer for 14 minutes. Turn the meatballs halfway through cooking. The beef meatballs should be browned on the outside and have an internal temperature of at least 80 °C when done. 3. Remove meatballs from fryer and toss in barbecue sauce. 4. Serve warm.
Per Serving: Calories 419; Fat 25g; Sodium 454mg; Carbs 6.3g; Fibre 0.3g; Sugar 2.5g; Protein 39.9g

Decadent Rosemary Lamb Chops

Prep Time: 5 minutes| **Cook Time:** 15 minutes| **Serves:** 4

8 (75 g) lamb chops
2 teaspoons extra-virgin olive oil
1½ teaspoons chopped fresh rosemary
1 garlic clove, minced
Salt
Pepper

1. Drizzle the 2 teaspoons of olive oil over the lamb chops. 2. Combine the rosemary, garlic, salt, and pepper in a small bowl. 3. Rub the seasoning onto the front and back of each lamb chop. 4. Place the lamb chops in the air fryer. (It is okay to stack them.) Cook for 10 minutes. 5. Open the air fryer. Flip the lamb chops. Cook for an additional 5 minutes. 6. Cool before serving.
Per serving: Calories 81; Fat 6.7g; Sodium 32mg; Carbs 1.4g; Fibre 0.2g; Sugar 0.6g; Protein 3.8g

Breaded Pork Chops

Prep Time: 5 minutes| **Cook Time:** 15 minutes| **Serves:** 5

5 (90 – 125 g) pork chops (bone-in or boneless)
Seasoning salt
Pepper
30 g plain flour
2 tablespoons panko bread crumbs
Cooking oil

1. Season the pork chops with the seasoning salt and pepper. 2. Sprinkle the flour on both sides of the pork chops, then coat both sides with panko bread crumbs. 3. Add the pork chops in the air fryer. It's okay to stack them. Spray the pork chops with cooking oil. Cook at 195 °C for 6 minutes. 4. Open the air fryer and then flip the pork chops. Cook for an additional 6 minutes. 5. Cool before serving.
Per Serving: Calories 134; Fat 36g; Sodium 105mg; Carbs 2.4g; Fibre 0.8g; Sugar 1.5g; Protein 9.7g

Beef and Mushroom Calzones

Prep Time: 10 minutes| **Cook Time:** 20 minutes| **Serves:** 6

Cooking oil
60 g chopped onion
2 garlic cloves, minced
20 g chopped mushrooms
455 g lean beef mince
1 tablespoon Italian seasoning
Salt
Pepper
380 g pizza sauce
1 teaspoon plain flour
1 (325 g) can refrigerated pizza dough
100 g shredded Cheddar cheese

1. Spray a frying pan with cooking oil and turn medium-high heat on. Add the chopped onion, garlic, and mushrooms. Cook them together for 2 to 3 minutes until fragrant. 2. Add the beef mince, Italian seasoning, salt, and pepper and break up the beef into small pieces with a large spoon. Cook the mixture for 2 to 4 minutes until the beef is browned. 3. Add the pizza sauce. Stir to combine. 4. Sprinkle the flour on a flat work surface. Roll out the pizza dough. Cut the dough into 6 equal-sized rectangles. 5. Mound some of the beef mince mixture on each of the rectangles. Sprinkle 1 tablespoon of shredded cheese over the beef mixture. 6. Fold each crust up to close the calzones. Press along and seal the open edges of each calzone with the back of a fork. 7. Place the calzones in the air fryer. Do not stack. Cook in batches. Spray the calzones with cooking oil. Cook at 205 °C for 10 minutes. 8. Remove the cooked calzones from the air fryer, then repeat step 7 for the remaining calzones. 9. Cool before serving.
Per Serving: Calories 393; Fat 18.5g; Sodium 750mg; Carbs 26.2g; Fibre 3.3g; Sugar 6g; Protein 29g

Savory Worcestershire Cheeseburgers

Prep Time: 5 minutes| **Cook Time:** 15 minutes| **Serves:** 4

455 g lean beef mince
1 teaspoon Worcestershire sauce
1 tablespoon burger seasoning
Salt
Pepper
Cooking oil
4 slices cheese
4 buns

1. Mix the beef mince, Worcestershire, burger seasoning, salt, and pepper in a large bowl. 2. Spray the cooking oil over the air fryer basket. (only a quick spritz, the burgers will produce oil as they cook.) 3. Shape the mixture into 4 patties. Place the burgers in the air fryer. Cook at 180 °C for 8 minutes. 4. Open the air fryer and then flip the burgers. Cook for an additional 3 to 4 minutes. 5. Stick a knife or fork in the centre to examine the colour to check the inside of the burgers when they are fully cooked. 6. Add one cheese slice on top of each burger. Cook in your air fryer for an additional minute, or until the cheese has melted. 7. Serve on buns with any additional toppings of your choice.
Per Serving: Calories 648; Fat 37g; Sodium 990mg; Carbs 37g; Fibre 1.2g; Sugar 20g; Protein 39g

Italian Parmesan Breaded Pork Chops

Prep Time: 5 minutes| **Cook Time:** 25 minutes| **Serves:** 5

5 (90 – 125 g) pork chops (bone-in or boneless)
1 teaspoon Italian seasoning
Seasoning salt
Pepper
30 g plain flour
2 tablespoons Italian bread crumbs
3 tablespoons finely grated Parmesan cheese
Cooking oil

1. Season the pork chops with the Italian seasoning, seasoning salt, and pepper. 2. Sprinkle the flour on both sides of the pork chops, then coat both sides with the bread crumbs and Parmesan cheese. 3. Add the pork chops to the air fryer. Stacking them. Spray the pork chops with cooking oil. Cook at 195 °C for 6 minutes. 4. Open the air fryer and then flip the pork chops. Cook for an additional 6 minutes. 5. Cool before serving.
Per Serving: Calories 148; Fat 4.7g; Sodium 200mg; Carbs 15.3g; Fibre 0.9g; Sugar 1.6g; Protein 10.6g

Air Fried Sausage, Peppers, and Onions

Prep Time: 5 minutes| **Cook Time:** 15 minutes| **Serves:** 5

5 Italian sausages
1 green pepper, cut into strips without seeds
1 red pepper, seeded and cut into strips
½ onion, cut into strips
1 teaspoon dried oregano
½ teaspoon garlic powder
5 Italian rolls or buns

1. Place the sausages in the air fryer. Cook at 180 °C for 10 minutes. 2. Season the green and red peppers and the onion with the oregano and garlic powder. 3. Open the air fryer and then flip the sausages. Add the peppers and onion to the basket. Cook them in your air fryer for an additional 3 to 5 minutes, until the vegetables are soft and the sausages are no longer pink on the inside. 4. Serve the sausages (sliced or whole) on buns with the peppers and onion.
Per Serving: Calories 521; Fat 37g; Sodium 1038mg; Carbs 25g; Fibre 1.5g; Sugar 4g; Protein 20.8g

Beef Taco Chimichangas

Prep Time: 10 minutes| **Cook Time:** 20 minutes| **Serves:** 4

Cooking oil
55 g chopped onion
2 garlic cloves, minced
455 g lean beef mince
2 tablespoons taco seasoning
Salt
Pepper
1 (375 g) can diced tomatoes with chiles
4 medium (20 cm) flour tortillas
100 g Cheddar cheese, shreded (a blend of 50 g shredded Cheddar and 50 g shredded Monterey Jack works great, too)

1. Spray a frying pan with cooking oil and turn medium-high heat on. Add chopped onion and garlic, cook for 2 to 3 minutes until fragrant. 2. Add beef mince, taco seasoning, salt, and pepper. Break up the beef with a spatula. Cook for 2 to 4 minutes until browned. 3. Add the diced tomatoes with chiles. Stir to combine. 4. Mound some of the beef mince mixture on each tortilla. 5. Fold the sides of the tortilla in toward the middle and then roll up from the bottom to form chimichangas. (You can secure the chimichanga with a toothpick. Or you can moisten the upper edge of the tortilla with a small amount of water before sealing. Use a cooking brush or dab with your fingers.) 6. Spray the chimichangas with cooking oil. Place the chimichangas in the air fryer. Do not stack. Cook in batches 205 °C for 8 minutes. 7. Remove the cooked chimichangas from the air fryer and top them with the shredded cheese. The heat from the chimichangas will melt the cheese. (Repeat the steps for the remaining chimichangas) 9. Serve.
Per Serving: Calories 494; Fat 16g; Sodium 1552mg; Carbs 49.5g; Fibre 6.5g; Sugar 16.18g; Protein 39.2g

Ham and Cheese Stromboli

Prep Time: 10 minutes| **Cook Time:** 20 minutes| **Serves:** 6

1 teaspoon plain flour
1 (325 g) can refrigerated pizza dough
6 slices provolone cheese
55 g shredded mozzarella cheese
12 slices deli ham
½ red pepper, seeded and sliced
½ teaspoon dried basil
½ teaspoon oregano
Pepper
Cooking oil

1. Sprinkle the flour on a flat work surface. Roll out the pizza dough. Cut the dough into 6 equal-sized rectangles. 2. Add 1 slice of provolone, 1 tablespoon of mozzarella, 2 slices of ham, and a few slices of red pepper to each rectangle. 3. Season each with dried basil, oregano, and pepper. 4. Fold up each crust to close the stromboli. Use the back of a fork to help press along and seal the open edges. 5. Place the stromboli in the air fryer. Do not stack. Cook in batches. Spray the stromboli with cooking oil and cook for 10 minutes. 6. Remove the cooked stromboli from the air fryer, then repeat step 5 for the remaining stromboli. 7. Cool before serving.
Per Serving: Calories 347; Fat 18.4g; Sodium 1355mg; Carbs 20g; Fibre 1.8g; Sugar 3g; Protein 25g

Sweet and Spicy Short Ribs

Prep Time: 65 minutes| **Cook Time:** 10 minutes| **Serves:** 4

8 (200 g) bone-in short ribs
120 ml soy sauce
60 ml rice wine vinegar
55 g chopped onion
2 garlic cloves, minced
1 tablespoon sesame oil
1 teaspoon Sriracha
4 spring onions, green parts (white parts optional), thinly sliced, divided
Salt
Pepper

1. Place the short ribs in a sealable plastic bag. Add soy sauce, rice wine vinegar, onion, garlic, sesame oil, Sriracha, and half of the spring onions. Season with salt and pepper. 2. Seal the plastic bag and place it in the refrigerator to marinate for at least 1 hour (overnight is optimal). 3. Place the short ribs in the air fryer. (Do not overfill. You may have to cook in two batches.) Cook for 4 minutes. 4. Open the air fryer and then flip the ribs. Cook for an additional 4 minutes. (If necessary, remove the cooked short ribs from the air fryer, then repeat steps 3 and 4 for the remaining ribs.) 5. Sprinkle the short ribs with the remaining spring onions, and serve.
Per Serving: Calories 258; Fat 15g; Sodium 522mg; Carbs 11g; Fibre 1.1g; Sugar 7.4g; Protein 18.5g

Juicy Steak Fajitas

Prep Time: 10 minutes| **Cook Time:** 10 minutes| **Serves:** 4 g

455 g beef flank steak, cut into strips
1 red pepper, cut into strips
1 green pepper, cut into strips
½ red onion, cut into strips
2 tablespoons taco or fajita seasoning
Salt
Pepper
2 tablespoons extra-virgin olive oil
8 medium (20 cm) flour tortillas

1. Combine beef, red and green peppers, onion, taco seasoning, salt, pepper, and olive oil in a large bowl. Mix them well. 2. Transfer the beef and vegetable mixture to the air fryer. It is okay to stack. Cook at 195 °C for 5 minutes. 3. Open the air fryer and shake the basket. Cook for an additional 4 to 5 minutes. 4. Divide the beef and vegetables evenly among the tortillas and serve with any of your desired additional toppings.
Per Serving: Calories 491; Fat 14.3g; Sodium 1098mg; Carbs 55g; Fibre 3.7g; Sugar 6g; Protein 32.8g

Roasted Pork Tenderloin

Prep Time: 5 minutes| **Cook Time:** 60 minutes| **Serves:** 6

1 (1.3 kg) pork tenderloin
2 tablespoons extra-virgin olive oil
2 garlic cloves, minced
1 teaspoon dried basil
1 teaspoon dried oregano
1 teaspoon dried thyme
Salt
Pepper

1. Drizzle the pork tenderloin with the olive oil. 2. Rub the garlic, basil, oregano, thyme, salt and pepper all over the tenderloin. 3. Place the tenderloin in the air fryer. Cook at 180 °C for 45 minutes. 4. Use a meat thermometer to test for doneness. 5. Open the air fryer and flip the pork tenderloin. Cook for an additional 15 minutes. 6. Remove the cooked pork from the air fryer and allow it to rest for 10 minutes before cutting.
Per Serving: Calories 348; Fat 10g; Sodium 170mg; Carbs 1g; Fibre 0.3g; Sugar 0.4g; Protein 59.6g

Swedish Meatballs

Prep Time: 10 minutes| **Cook Time:** 20 minutes| **Serves:** 10

For the meatballs
455 g lean beef mince
1 (25 g) packet Onion Soup Mix
35 g bread crumbs
1 egg, beaten
Salt
Pepper
For the gravy
240 ml beef stock
70 g heavy cream
2 tablespoons plain flour

To make the meatballs
1. Combine the beef mince, onion soup mix, bread crumbs, egg, salt, and pepper in a large bowl. Mix thoroughly. 2. Use gloves to assemble the meatballs. Use 2 tablespoons of the meat mixture to create each meatball, rolling the beef mixture around in your hands. Yield about 10 meatballs. 3. Place the beef meatballs in the air fryer. It is okay to stack them. Cook at 185 °C for 14 minutes.
To make the gravy
1. Prepare the gravy while the meatballs are cooking. Heat a saucepan over medium-high heat. 2. Add the beef stock and heavy cream. Stir for 1 to 2 minutes. 3. Add the flour and stir. Then simmer the sauce for 3 to 4 minutes, or until thickened. 4. Drizzle the gravy over the meatballs and serve.
Per Serving: Calories 135; Fat 7.5g; Sodium 46mg; Carbs 2.6g; Fibre 0.2g; Sugar 0.6g; Protein 13.4g

Marinated Steak Kebabs

Prep Time: 45 minutes| **Cook Time:** 5 minutes| **Serves:** 4

450 g strip steak, fat trimmed, cut into 2.5 cm cubes
120 ml soy sauce
60 ml olive oil
1 tablespoon granular brown sweetener
½ teaspoon salt
¼ teaspoon ground black pepper
1 medium green pepper, chopped into 2.5 cm cubes without seeds

1. Place the steak into a large sealable bowl or bag, pour in soy sauce and olive oil, add sweetener, then stir them to coat the steak. 2. Marinate the steak at room temperature for 30 minutes (or in the refrigerator for 24 hours). 3. Remove steak from marinade and sprinkle with salt and black pepper. 4. Chop the steak into 2.5 cm cubes. 5. Place them and vegetables onto 15 cm skewer sticks, alternating between steak and pepper. 6. Place kebabs into an ungreased air fryer basket. Adjust the temperature setting to 205 °C and set the timer for 5 minutes. It will be done when the meat edges are crispy and peppers are tender. 8. Serve warm.
Per Serving: Calories 457; Fat 31g; Sodium 1296mg; Carbs 9g; Fibre 0.9g; Sugar 7g; Protein 35g

Ribeye Steak

Prep Time: 5 minutes| **Cook Time:** 20 minutes| **Serves:** 4

4 (200 g) ribeye steaks
1 tablespoon Steak Seasoning
Salt
Pepper

1. Season the steaks with the steak seasoning, salt, and pepper. 2. Place 2 steaks in the air fryer. Cook at 180 °C for 4 minutes . 3. Open the air fryer and then flip the steaks. Cook for an additional 4 to 5 minutes. 4. Check for doneness to determine how much additional cook time is need. (Check the level of pink with a fork. Or use a meat thermometer) 5. Remove the cooked steaks from the air fryer, then repeat steps 2-4 for the remaining 2 steaks. 6. Cool before serving.
Per Serving: Calories 117; Fat 6.5g; Sodium 206mg; Carbs 3.3g; Fibre 0.5g; Sugar 0.8g; Protein 11.4g

Classic Southern Chicken-Fried Steak

Prep Time: 10 minutes| **Cook Time:** 15 minutes| **Serves:** 4

For the steak
60 g plain flour
Seasoning salt
Pepper
Cooking oil
2 eggs
80 g panko bread crumbs
4 (100 g) cube steaks
For the gravy
1 (20 g) package Gravy Mix
480 ml water

To make the steak
1. Combine the flour, seasoning salt, and pepper in a bowl. 2. Spray the air fryer basket with cooking oil. 3. Beat the eggs in a small bowl. In a second bowl, place in the panko bread crumbs. 4. Dip each steak in the flour, then the eggs, and then the bread crumbs. 5. Place the steaks in the air fryer. Do not stack. Cook in batches. Spray the top of the steaks with cooking oil. Cook at 185 °C for 7 minutes. 6. Remove the cooked steaks from the air fryer, then repeat step 5 for the remaining steaks.
To make the gravy
1. Prepare the gravy while the steaks are cooking. Place a saucepan over medium heat. Add the gravy mix. 2. Slowly add water to the pan. Stir frequently until the mix boils. Reduce heat and simmer for 1 minute. The sauce will thicken upon standing. Drizzle the gravy over the steaks, and serve.
Per Serving: Calories 178; Fat 6g; Sodium 145mg; Carbs 17g; Fibre 0.8g; Sugar 1g; Protein 13g

Barbecued Baby Back Ribs

Prep Time: 35 minutes| **Cook Time:** 30 minutes| **Serves:** 4

1 rack baby back ribs
1 teaspoon onion powder
1 teaspoon garlic powder
1 teaspoon brown sugar
1 teaspoon dried oregano
Salt
Pepper
125 g barbecue sauce

1. Remove the thin membrane part from the back baby ribs with a sharp knife. Cut the rack in half or as needed so that the ribs are able to fit in the air fryer. 2. Combine the onion powder, garlic powder, brown sugar, oregano, salt and pepper in a small bowl. Rub the seasoning onto the front and back of the ribs. 3. Cover the ribs with plastic wrap or foil and allow them to sit at room temperature for 30 minutes. 4. Place the ribs in the air fryer. It is okay to stack them. Cook for 15 minutes. 5. Open the air fryer. Flip the ribs. Cook for an additional 15 minutes. 6. Transfer the ribs to a serving dish. Drizzle the barbecue sauce over the ribs and serve.
Per Serving: Calories 375; Fat 2g; Sodium 474mg; Carbs 13g; Fibre 0.8g; Sugar 0.6g; Protein 18g

Mozzarella Corn Dogs Mozzarella

Prep Time: 10 minutes| **Cook Time:** 8 minutes| **Serves:** 4

170 g shredded mozzarella cheese
25 g cream cheese
50 g blanched finely ground almond flour
4 beef hot dogs

1. Place mozzarella, cream cheese, and flour in a large microwave-safe bowl. 2. Microwave them on high for 45 seconds, then stir with a fork until a soft ball of dough forms. 3. Press dough out into a 30 cm × 15 cm rectangle, then use a knife to separate into four smaller rectangles. 4. Wrap each hot dog in one rectangular dough and place into ungreased air fryer basket. 5. Adjust the temperature to 205 °C and set the timer for 8 minutes(turning corn dogs halfway through cooking). 6. Corn dogs will be golden brown when done. 7. Serve warm.
Per Serving: Calories 299; Fat 21g; Sodium 843mg; Carbs 16g; Fibre 2.5g; Sugar 1.5g; Protein 14.4g

Pork Tenderloin with Mustard

Prep Time: 5 minutes| **Cook Time:** 20 minutes| **Serves:** 6

55 g mayonnaise
2 tablespoons Dijon mustard
½ teaspoon dried thyme
¼ teaspoon dried rosemary
1 (450 g) pork tenderloin
½ teaspoon salt
¼ teaspoon ground black pepper

1. Mix mayonnaise, mustard, thyme, and rosemary in a small bowl. 2. Brush tenderloin with mixture on all sides, then sprinkle with salt and pepper on all sides. 3. Place tenderloin into an ungreased air fryer basket. 4. Adjust the temperature setting to 205 °C and set the timer for 20 minutes, turning tenderloin halfway through cooking. 5. Tenderloin will be golden and have an internal temperature of at least 60 °C when done. 6. Serve warm.
Per Serving: Calories 144; Fat 6g; Sodium 372mg; Carbs 0.8g; Fibre 0.4g; Sugar 0.2g; Protein 20.6g

Wrapped Pork Tenderloin

Prep Time: 10 minutes| **Cook Time:** 20 minutes| **Serves:** 6

1 (450 g) pork tenderloin
½ teaspoon salt
½ teaspoon garlic powder
¼ teaspoon ground black pepper
8 slices sugar-free bacon

1. Sprinkle tenderloin with salt, garlic powder, and pepper. 2. Wrap each piece of bacon around tenderloin and secure it with toothpicks.3. Place tenderloin into an ungreased air fryer basket. 4. Adjust the temperature setting to 205 °C and set the timer for 20 minutes, turning tenderloin after 15 minutes. Bacon will be crispy and tenderloin will have an internal temperature of at least 60 °C when done. 5. Cut the tenderloin into six even portions and transfer each to a medium plate. 6. Serve warm.
Per Serving: Calories 110; Fat 2.66g; Sodium 237mg; Carbs 0.37g; Fibre 0.1g; Sugar 0.1g; Protein 20g

Butter Pork Chops

Prep Time: 5 minutes| **Cook Time:** 12 minutes| **Serves:** 4

4 (100 g) boneless pork chops
½ teaspoon salt
¼ teaspoon ground black pepper
2 tablespoons salted butter, softened

1. Sprinkle pork chops on all sides with salt and pepper. 2. Place chops into an ungreased air fryer basket in a single layer. 3. Adjust the temperature setting to 205 °C and set the timer for 12 minutes. 4. Pork chops will be golden and have an internal temperature of at least 60 °C when done. 5. Use tongs to remove cooked pork chops from your air fryer and place onto a large plate. 6. Top each chop with ½ tablespoon butter and sit for 2 minutes to melt. 7. Serve warm.
Per Serving: Calories 71; Fat 4.79g; Sodium 5185mg; Carbs 0.3g; Fibre 0g; Sugar 0g; Protein 6.5g

Pork Chops Stuffed with Bacon and Cheese

Prep Time: 10 minutes| **Cook Time:** 12 minutes| **Serves:** 4

20 g grated parmesan cheese
50 g shredded sharp Cheddar cheese
4 slices cooked sugar-free bacon, crumbled
4 (100 g) boneless pork chops
½ teaspoon salt
¼ teaspoon ground black pepper

1. Mix parmesan, cheddar cheese, and bacon in a small bowl. 2. Make a 8 cm slit in the side of each pork chop and stuff with ¼ parmesan mixture. 3. Sprinkle each side of pork chops with salt and pepper. 4. Place pork chops into an ungreased air fryer basket, stuffed side up. 5. Adjust the temperature to 205 °C and set the timer for 12 minutes. Pork chops will be browned and have an internal temperature of at least 60 °C when done. 6. Serve warm.
Per Serving: Calories 321; Fat 18g; Sodium 723mg; Carbs 1g; Fibre 0g; Sugar 0g; Protein 37g

Parmesan-Crusted Pork Chops

Prep Time: 5 minutes| **Cook Time:** 12 minutes| **Serves:** 4

1 large egg
50 g grated Parmesan cheese
4 (100 g) boneless pork chops
½ teaspoon salt
¼ teaspoon ground black pepper

1. Whisk egg in a medium bowl and place Parmesan in a separate medium bowl. 2. Sprinkle pork chops on both sides with salt and pepper. 3. Dip each pork chop into egg, then press both sides into Parmesan. 4. Place pork chops into an ungreased air fryer basket. 5. Adjust the temperature to 205 °C and set the timer for 12 minutes, turning chops halfway through cooking. Pork chops will be golden and have an internal temperature of at least 60 °C when done. Serve warm.
Per Serving: Calories 302; Fat 10.94g; Sodium 609mg; Carbs 2.16g; Fibre 0g; Sugar 0.18g; Protein 45.74g

Roast Beef

Prep Time: 5 minutes| **Cook Time:** 60 minutes| **Serves:** 6

1 (900 g) top round beef roast
1 teaspoon salt
½ teaspoon ground black pepper
1 teaspoon dried rosemary
½ teaspoon garlic powder
1 tablespoon coconut oil, melted

1. Sprinkle all sides of roast with salt, pepper, rosemary, and garlic powder. 2. Drizzle with coconut oil. 3. Place roast into an ungreased air fryer basket, fatty side down. 4. Adjust the temperature setting to 190 °C and set the timer for 60 minutes, turning the roast halfway through cooking. Roast will be done when no pink remains and internal temperature is at least 80 °C. 5. Serve warm.
Per Serving: Calories 217; Fat 9g; Sodium 479mg; Carbs 0.6g; Fibre 0.1g; Sugar 0.2g; Protein 34g

Mexican Shredded Beef

Prep Time: 5 minutes| **Cook Time:** 35 minutes| **Serves:** 6

1 (900 g) beef chuck roast, cut into 5 cm cubes
1 teaspoon salt
½ teaspoon ground black pepper
125 g added chipotle sauce

1. Sprinkle the beef cubes with salt and pepper and toss to coat in a large bowl. 2. Place beef into an ungreased air fryer basket. 3. Adjust the temperature setting to 205 °C and set the timer for 30 minutes, shaking the basket halfway through cooking. Beef will be done when internal temperature is at least 70 °C. 4. Place cooked beef into a large bowl and shred with two forks. 5. Pour in chipotle sauce and toss to coat. 6. Return beef to air fryer basket for an additional 5 minutes at 205 °C to crisp with sauce. 7. Serve warm.
Per Serving: Calories 278; Fat 12.8g; Sodium 509mg; Carbs 0.35g; Fibre 0.1g; Sugar 0.19g; Protein 40.37g

Air Fried Worcestershire Pork Belly

Prep Time: 40 minutes| **Cook Time:** 20 minutes| **Serves:** 4

450 g pork belly, cut into 2.5 cm cubes
60 ml soy sauce
1 tablespoon Worcestershire sauce
2 teaspoons sriracha hot chili sauce
½ teaspoon salt
¼ teaspoon ground black pepper

1. Place pork belly into a medium sealable bowl or bag and pour in soy sauce, Worcestershire sauce, and sriracha. 2. Seal it and let it marinate for 30 minutes in the refrigerator. 3. Remove pork from marinade, pat dry with a paper towel, and sprinkle with salt and pepper. 4. Place pork in ungreased air fryer basket, adjust the temperature to 180 °C and set the timer for 20 minutes, shaking the basket halfway through cooking. 5. Pork belly will be done when it has an internal temperature of at least 60 °C and is golden brown. 6. Rest pork belly on a large plate 10 minutes. 7. Serve warm.

Per Serving: Calories 188; Fat 9g; Sodium 1851mg; Carbs 6.77g; Fibre 0.4g; Sugar 5.3g; Protein 20.5g

Tender Pork Spare Ribs

Prep Time: 10 minutes| **Cook Time:** 30 minutes| **Serves:** 4

1 (1.8 kg) rack pork spare ribs
1 teaspoon ground cumin
1 teaspoon ground black pepper
1 teaspoon garlic powder
½ teaspoon dry ground mustard
2 teaspoons salt
125 g low-carb barbecue sauce

1. Place ribs on the ungreased aluminum foil sheet, and carefully use a knife to remove membrane. 2. Sprinkle meat evenly on both sides with cumin, salt, pepper, garlic powder, and ground mustard. 3. Cut the rack pork spare ribs into portions to fit in your air fryer, and wrap each portion in a layer of aluminum foil, working in batches if needed. 4. Place ribs into an ungreased air fryer basket, adjust the temperature to 205 °C and set the timer for 25 minutes. 5. Carefully remove ribs from foil when the timer beeps and brush with barbecue sauce. 6. Return them to your air fryer and cook at 205 °C for an additional 5 minutes to brown. The cooking is done when no pink remains on the ribs and the internal temperature is at least 80 °C. Serve warm.

Per Serving: Calories 192; Fat 12g; Sodium 1344mg; Carbs 3g; Fibre 0g; Sugar 0g; Protein 13g

Spicy Pork Spare Ribs

Prep Time: 10 minutes| **Cook Time:** 30 minutes| **Serves:** 6

10 g granular brown sweetener
2 teaspoons paprika
2 teaspoons chili powder
1 teaspoon garlic powder
½ teaspoon cayenne pepper
2 teaspoons salt
1 teaspoon ground black pepper
1 (1.8 kg) rack pork spare ribs

1. Mix sweetener, paprika, chili powder, garlic powder, cayenne pepper, salt, and black pepper in a small bowl. 2. Rub spice mix over ribs on both sides. 3. Place ribs on ungreased aluminum foil sheet and wrap to cover. 4. Place ribs into an ungreased air fryer basket., adjust the temperature to 205 °C and set the timer for 25 minutes. 5. When timer beeps, remove ribs from foil, then place back into the air fryer basket to cook for an additional 5 minutes, turning halfway through cooking. Ribs will be browned and have an internal temperature of at least 80 °C when done. 6. Serve warm.

Per Serving: Calories 460; Fat 19g; Sodium 1165mg; Carbs 2g; Fibre 0.8g; Sugar 0g; Protein 66g

Italian Beef Meatballs

Prep Time: 10 minutes| **Cook Time:** 20 minutes| **Serves:** 4

450 g beef mince
1 large egg, whisked
25 g grated Parmesan cheese
½ teaspoon salt
½ teaspoon dried parsley
¼ teaspoon ground black pepper
¼ teaspoon dried oregano

1. Combine beef mince, the whisked egg, Parmesan cheese, salt, parsley, black pepper, and oregano in a large bowl. 2. Scoop out 3 tablespoons mixture and roll into a ball. 3. Repeat with remaining mixture to form sixteen balls total. 4. Place meatballs into an ungreased air fryer basket in a single layer, working in batches if needed. 5. Adjust the temperature to 205 °C and set the timer for 20 minutes, shaking the basket halfway through cooking. 6. Meatballs will be browned and have an internal temperature of at least 80 °C when done.7. Serve warm.
Per Serving: Calories 284; Fat 15g; Sodium 475mg; Carbs 1g; Fibre 0g; Sugar 0g; Protein 33g

Pork Meatballs

Prep Time: 10 minutes| **Cook Time:** 12 minutes| **Serves:** 6

450 g pork mince
1 large egg, whisked
½ teaspoon garlic powder
½ teaspoon salt
½ teaspoon ground ginger
¼ teaspoon crushed red pepper flakes
1 medium spring onion, trimmed and sliced

1. Combine the pork mince, the whisked egg, garlic powder, salt, ginger, pepper flakes, and spring onion in a large bowl. 2. Spoon out 2 tablespoons mixture and roll into a ball, repeat to form eighteen meatballs total. 3. Place meatballs into an ungreased air fryer basket. 4. Adjust the temperature setting to 205 °C and set the timer for 12 minutes, shaking the basket three times throughout cooking. Meatballs will be browned and have an internal temperature of at least 60 °C when done. 5. Serve warm.
Per Serving: Calories 164; Fat 10g; Sodium 252mg; Carbs 1g; Fibre 0g; Sugar 0g; Protein 15g

London Steak

Prep Time: 2 hours | **Cook Time:** 12 minutes| **Serves:** 4

450 g top round steak
1 tablespoon Worcestershire sauce
60 ml soy sauce
2 cloves garlic, peeled and finely minced
½ teaspoon ground black pepper
½ teaspoon salt
2 tablespoons salted butter, melted

1. Place steak in a large sealable bowl or bag, pour in Worcestershire sauce and soy sauce, then add garlic, pepper, and salt, and toss to coat. 2. Seal it and place it into a refrigerator to marinate for 2 hours. 3. Remove steak from marinade and pat dry. 4. Drizzle top side with butter, then place into ungreased air fryer basket. 5. Adjust the temperature to 190 °C and set the timer for 12 minutes, turning steak halfway through cooking. 6. Steak will be done when browned at the edges and it has an internal temperature of 65 °C for medium or 80 °C for well-done. 7. Rest the steak on a large plate for 10 minutes before slicing into thin pieces. 8. Serve warm.
Per Serving: Calories 271; Fat 11g; Sodium 691mg; Carbs 6g; Fibre 0g; Sugar 4g; Protein 35g

Spice-Rubbed Pork Loin

Prep Time: 5 minutes| **Cook Time:** 20 minutes| **Serves:** 6

1 teaspoon paprika
½ teaspoon ground cumin
½ teaspoon chili powder
½ teaspoon garlic powder
2 tablespoons coconut oil
1 (675 g) boneless pork loin
½ teaspoon salt
¼ teaspoon ground black pepper

1. Mix paprika, cumin, chili powder, and garlic powder in a small bowl. 2. Drizzle coconut oil over pork. 3. Sprinkle pork loin with salt and pepper, then rub spice mixture evenly on all sides. 4. Place pork loin into an ungreased air fryer basket. 5. Adjust the temperature to 205 °C and set the timer for 20 minutes, turning pork halfway through cooking. Pork loin will be browned and have an internal temperature of at least 60 °C when done. 6. Serve warm.

Per Serving: Calories 193; Fat 9g; Sodium 257mg; Carbs 1g; Fibre 0g; Sugar 0g; Protein 26g

Tender Blackened Steak Nuggets

Prep Time: 10 minutes| **Cook Time:** 7 minutes| **Serves:** 2

450 g ribeye steak, cut into 2.5 cm cubes
2 tablespoons salted butter, melted
½ teaspoon paprika
½ teaspoon salt
¼ teaspoon garlic powder
¼ teaspoon onion powder
¼ teaspoon ground black pepper
⅛ teaspoon cayenne pepper

1. Place the steak into a large bowl and pour in butter, then toss to coat. 2. Sprinkle with the remaining ingredients. 3. Place steak into an ungreased air fryer basket. 4. Adjust the temperature to 205 °C and set the timer for 7 minutes, shaking the basket three times during cooking. Steak will be crispy on the outside and browned when done and internal temperature is at least 65 °C for medium and 80 °C for well-done. 5. Serve warm.

Per Serving: Calories 498; Fat 34g; Sodium 844mg; Carbs 5.4g; Fibre 0.4g; Sugar 0.4g; Protein 44.5g

Marinated Ribeye Steak

Prep Time: 35 minutes| **Cook Time:** 10 minutes| **Serves:** 4

450 g ribeye steak
60 ml soy sauce
1 tablespoon Worcestershire sauce
1 tablespoon granular brown sweetener
2 tablespoons olive oil
½ teaspoon salt
¼ teaspoon ground black pepper

1. Place ribeye in a large sealable bowl or bag and pour in soy sauce, Worcestershire sauce, sweetener, and olive oil. 2. Seal it and marinate it for 30 minutes in the refrigerator. 3. Remove ribeye from marinade, pat dry, and sprinkle on all sides with salt and pepper. 4. Place ribeye into an ungreased air fryer basket, adjust the temperature to 205 °C, and set the timer for 10 minutes. Steak will be done when browned at the edges and has an internal temperature of 65 °C for medium or 80 °C for well-done. Serve warm.

Per Serving: Calories 333; Fat 23g; Sodium 733mg; Carbs 7.2g; Fibre 0.4g; Sugar 3.6g; Protein 24g

Mozzarella-Stuffed Meatloaf

Prep Time: 10 minutes| **Cook Time:** 30 minutes| **Serves:** 6

450 g lean beef
½ medium green pepper, seeded and chopped
¼ medium yellow onion, peeled and chopped
½ teaspoon salt
¼ teaspoon ground black pepper
50 g mozzarella cheese, sliced into ½ cm thick slices
60 g ketchup

1. Combine beef mince, pepper, onion, salt, and black pepper in a large bowl. 2. Cut a suitable piece of parchment to fit your air fryer basket and place the half beef mixture on ungreased parchment (form a 23 cm × 10 cm loaf, about 1 cm thick). 3. Centre mozzarella slices on the beef loaf (leaving at least ½ cm around each edge). 4. Press the remaining beef into a second 23 cm × 10 cm loaf and place it on top of the mozzarella slices, and press the edges of the two loaves together to seal. 5. Place the meatloaf with parchment into the air fryer basket. Adjust the temperature setting to 175 °C and set the timer for 30 minutes. 6. Carefully turn over the loaf and brush the top with ketchup halfway through cooking. 7. Loaf will be browned and have an internal temperature of at least 80 °C when done. 8. Slice and serve warm.
Per Serving: Calories 178; Fat 8.4g; Sodium 318mg; Carbs 1g; Fibre 0.3g; Sugar 0.6g; Protein 23g

Cheese-Stuffed Steak Burgers

Prep Time: 10 minutes| **Cook Time:** 10 minutes| **Serves:** 4

450 g sirloin mince
100 g mild Cheddar cheese, cubed
½ teaspoon salt
¼ teaspoon ground black pepper

1. Form sirloin mince into four equal balls, separate each ball in half and flatten into two thin patties (eight total patties). 2. Add 25 g Cheddar cheese into the centre of one patty and top with a second patty, press edges to seal the burger closed. 3. Repeat with remaining patties and Cheddar to create four burgers. 4. Sprinkle salt and pepper over both sides of burgers and carefully place burgers into ungreased air fryer basket. 5. Adjust the temperature setting to 175 °C and set the timer for 10 minutes. 6. Burgers will be done when the edges and top are browned. 7. Serve warm.
Per Serving: Calories 218 ; Fat 11g; Sodium 669mg; Carbs 3.3g; Fibre 0g; Sugar 2.15g; Protein 26.15g

Parmesan Cheese Aubergine Sticks

Prep Time: 10 minutes| **Cook Time:** 24 minutes| **Serves:** 4

2 large eggs
2 tablespoons heavy cream
50 g grated Parmesan cheese
½ teaspoon salt
1 medium aubergine, cut into 1 cm rounds, then sliced into sticks
130 g no-sugar-added marinara sauce, warmed

1. Preheat air fryer to 205 °C for 3 minutes. 2. Whisk together eggs and heavy cream in a medium bowl. 3. Combine Parmesan cheese, and salt in a separate shallow dish. 4. Dip aubergine sticks in egg mixture. 5. Dredge it in parmesan mixture. 6. Place half of the aubergine sticks in air fryer basket lightly greased with olive oil. Cook for 6 minutes, then flip it and cook for another 6 minutes. 7. Repeat with remaining aubergine sticks. 8. Transfer it to a large serving plate and serve it with warmed marinara sauce for dipping.
Per Serving: Calories 140; Fat 8.76g; Sodium 526mg; Carbs 10.31g; Fibre 4.1g; Sugar 0g; Protein 6.4g

Simple Low-Carb Honey Mustard

Prep Time: 10 minutes| **Cook Time:** 0 minutes| **Serves:** 36

60 g mayonnaise
2 tablespoons yellow mustard
1 teaspoon Dijon mustard
¼ teaspoon apple cider vinegar
1 tablespoon granular sweetener

1. Combine all ingredients in a small bowl. 2. Refrigerate it for five days until ready to use.
Per Serving (1 teaspoon): Calories 7; Fat 0.64g; Sodium 31mg; Carbs 0.13g; Fibre 0.1g; Sugar 0.03g; Protein 0.25g

Roasted Avocado Shishito Peppers

Prep Time: 5 minutes| **Cook Time:** 10 minutes| **Serves:** 2

1 (100 g) bag shishito peppers, whole, rinsed and dried
1 tablespoon avocado oil, plus more for the basket
1 tablespoon minced garlic
Salt

1. Preheat the air fryer to 205 °C. 2. Toss the shishitos with the avocado oil, garlic, and salt in a medium bowl. 3. Lightly spritz the air fryer basket with oil. 4. Place the shishitos in the basket. 4. Air fry at 205 °C for 8 to 10 minutes, shaking the basket every 3 to 4 minutes to ensure even cooking. 5. Make sure the peppers are roasted and blistered, but not burned.
Per Serving: Calories 68; Fat 7.02g; Sodium 1mg; Carbs 1.41g; Fibre 0.1g; Sugar 0.04g; Protein 0.27g

Italian Crispy Stuffed Olives

Prep Time: 15 minutes| **Cook Time:** 10 minutes| **Serves:** 6

1 (250 g) jar garlic- or pimento-stuffed olives
30 g plain flour
1 large egg
110 g Italian seasoned panko bread crumbs
Extra-virgin olive oil, for spraying

1. Preheat the air fryer to 205 °C. 2. Remove the olives from the jar and dry them completely with paper towels. 3. Add the flour to a small shallow bowl. Beat the egg in a second small shallow bowl. Put the bread crumbs in a third small shallow bowl. 4. Toss the olives in the flour. 5. Coat each olive in the beaten egg, then in the breading. 6. Lightly spray the air fryer basket with oil, place the coated olives in a single layer in the basket, and lightly spray with oil. 7. Air fry at 205 °C for 6 to 8 minutes, shaking the basket gently after 2 minutes to ensure even cooking. 7. Serve it hot.
Per Serving: Calories 44; Fat 1.07g; Sodium 37mg; Carbs 6.98g; Fibre 0.3g; Sugar 0.36g; Protein 1.51g

Air-Fryer Vegetable Dumplings with Dipping Sauce

Prep Time: 30 minutes| **Cook Time:** 20 minutes| **Serves:** 4

For the dumplings
1 tablespoon extra-virgin olive oil, plus more for spraying
1 (200 g) box cremini mushrooms, finely chopped
2 teaspoons minced garlic
1 teaspoon grated fresh ginger
1 (350 g) bag coleslaw mix, refrigerated
1 (300 g) package round dumpling wrappers
For the dipping sauce
1 tablespoon soy sauce
2 teaspoons rice vinegar
1 teaspoon sesame oil
½ tablespoon packed brown sugar

To make the dumplings: 1. Set the heat to medium and then add olive oil in a 25 cm frying pan. Add the mushrooms, garlic, and ginger and sauté for 2 to 3 minutes, and add the coleslaw mix and sauté for another 4 to 5 minutes, or until the coleslaw is soft. 2. Stir the vegetables frequently and cook it until all the moisture has evaporated and the mixture is dry. 3. Place 2 teaspoons of vegetable filling in the centre of each dumpling wrapper. 4. Moisten the edges of the dumpling wrapper with water. Fold over the wrapper and seal the edges with your fingers, making pleats and pinching the edges to close them well. 5. Preheat the air fryer to 185 °C. Lightly spray the air fryer basket with oil, and place the dumplings in a single layer in the basket. (Air fry in batches, if necessary.) Don't forget to lightly spray with oil. 6. Air fry at 185 °C for 6 minutes. 7. Flip the dumplings and lightly spray with oil. 8. Air fry for another 6 minutes, or until it's golden brown and crispy.
To make the dipping sauce: 1. While the dumplings are air frying, combine the soy sauce, rice vinegar, sesame oil, and brown sugar in a small bowl, and stir them until the sugar dissolves. 2. Serve the dumplings with the dipping sauce.
Per Serving: Calories 162; Fat 5.27g; Sodium 68mg; Carbs 29.22g; Fibre 0.2g; Sugar 27.5g; Protein 0.5g

Fried Cinnamon Apple Chips

Prep Time: 10 minutes| **Cook Time:** 10 minutes| **Serves:** 4

Olive oil
2 apples, any variety, cored, cut in half, and cut into thin slices
2 heaped teaspoons ground cinnamon

1. Spray an air fryer basket lightly with oil. 2. Toss the apple slices with the cinnamon until evenly coated in a medium bowl. 3. Place the apple slices in the fryer basket in a single layer, and cook them in batches. 4. Air fry at 175 °C for 4 to 5 minutes. 5. Shake the basket and cook until crispy, for another 4 to 5 minutes.
Per Serving: Calories 3; Fat 0.02g; Sodium 0mg; Carbs 1.05g; Fibre 0.7g; Sugar 0.03g; Protein 0.05g

Spicy Fried Buffalo Chicken Dip

Prep Time: 10 minutes| **Cook Time:** 10 minutes| **Serves:** 4

140 g cooked, diced chicken breast
200 g full-fat cream cheese, softened
120 g buffalo sauce
80 ml full-fat ranch dressing
85 g chopped pickled jalapeños
150 g shredded medium Cheddar cheese, divided
2 spring onions, sliced on the bias

1. Place chicken into a large bowl. 2. Add the dressing, sauce, and cheese in it. 3. Stir them until the sauces are well mixed and mostly smooth. 4. Fold in jalapeños and 100 g Cheddar. 5. Pour the mixture into a 15 cm x 5cm baking dish and place remaining Cheddar on top. 6. Place dish into the air fryer basket. 7. Adjust the temperature to 175 °C and set the timer for 10 minutes. 8. When done, the top will be brown and the dip bubbling. 9. Top it with sliced spring onions. 10. Serve it warm.
Per Serving: Calories 276; Fat 16.12g; Sodium 939mg; Carbs 28.61g; Fibre 0.4g; Sugar 19.24g; Protein 4.97g

Simple Avocado Fries with Dipping Sauce

Prep Time: 20 minutes| **Cook Time:** 10 minutes| **Serves:** 6

For the avocado fries
4 slightly underripe avocados, halved and pitted
160 g panko bread crumbs
¾ teaspoon freshly ground black pepper
1½ teaspoons paprika
¾ teaspoon salt
3 large eggs
Extra-virgin olive oil, for spraying
For the dipping sauce
115 g sour cream
115 g mayonnaise
2 to 3 teaspoons sriracha
½ teaspoon freshly squeezed lemon juice

To make the avocado fries: 1. To prepare, heat your air fryer to 175 °C. 2. Carefully remove the skin from the avocados while leaving the flesh intact. 3. Cut each avocado in half lengthwise into 5 to 6 slices, and set it aside. 4. Mix together the bread crumbs, pepper, paprika, and salt in a small shallow bowl. 4. Whisk the eggs in a second small shallow bowl. 5. Coat each avocado slice in the eggs, then in the bread crumbs. Press on the bread crumbs to ensure they adhere. 6. Lightly spray the air fryer basket with oil. 87 Place the avocado fries in a single layer in the basket. 8. Lightly spray with oil. Air fry the avocado fries at 175 °C for 3 to 4 minutes. 9. Gently flip the fries and lightly spray with oil. Air fry for another 3 to 4 minutes, or until golden brown and crispy.
To make the dipping sauce: 1. While they're cooking, combine the sour cream, mayonnaise, sriracha, and lemon juice in a small bowl. 2. Serve it with the fries immediately.
Per Serving: Calories 359; Fat 30.69g; Sodium 519mg; Carbs 18.58g; Fibre 9.6g; Sugar 1.9g; Protein 6.8g

Fried Cinnamon and Sugar Peaches

Prep Time: 10 minutes| **Cook Time:** 13 minutes| **Serves:** 4

Olive oil
2 tablespoons sugar
¼ teaspoon ground cinnamon
4 peaches, cut into wedges

1. Spray an air fryer basket lightly with olive oil. 2. In a medium bowl combine together the sugar and cinnamon, and then add the peaches and toss to coat evenly. 3. Place the peaches in a single layer in the fryer basket on their sides, and cook them in batches. 4. Air fry at 175 °C for 5 minutes. 5. Turn the peaches skin side down, lightly spray them with oil, and air fry until the peaches are lightly brown and caramelized, for 5 to 8 more minutes.
Per Serving: Calories 74; Fat 0g; Sodium 0mg; Carbs 18g; Fibre 2g; Sugar 16.5g; Protein 1.4g

Mini Sweet Pepper Bacon Poppers

Prep Time: 15 minutes| **Cook Time:** 8 minutes| **Serves:** 4

8 mini sweet peppers
200 g full-fat cream cheese, softened
4 slices bacon, cooked and crumbled
30 g shredded pepper jack cheese

1. Remove the tops from the peppers and slice each one in half lengthwise. 2. Use a small knife to remove seeds and membranes. 3. Mix cream cheese, bacon, and pepper jack in a small bowl. 4. Place 3 teaspoons of the mixture into each sweet pepper and press it down smooth. Place into the air fryer basket. 5. Adjust the temperature to 205 °C and set the timer for 8 minutes. 6. Serve it warm.
Per Serving: Calories 233; Fat 11.12g; Sodium 336mg; Carbs 25.98g; Fibre 3.3g; Sugar 1.69g; Protein 10.86g

Air-fryer Raspberry Brie

Prep Time: 15 minutes| **Cook Time:** 15 minutes| **Serves:** 6

1 tablespoon plain flour
1 puff pastry sheet, at room temperature
1 (200 g) Brie wheel, refrigerated
80 g raspberry preserves
2 tablespoons fresh raspberries
1 large egg
1 tablespoon water
Extra-virgin olive oil, for the basket

1. Preheat the air fryer to 175 °C. 2. Dust your work surface with the flour, then roll out the puff pastry sheet. 3. Cut the rind off the Brie and discard it, and place the Brie in the centre of the puff pastry sheet. 4. Spread the raspberry preserves on top of the Brie, and then sprinkle the fresh raspberries on top. 5. Fold up the sides of the puff pastry around the Brie, and press the seams of the pastry together until they are closed. 6. Whisk together the egg and water in a small bowl, and brush the egg wash all over the top and sides of the puff pastry.7. Generously spritz the air fryer basket with oil, and place the pastry-enrobed Brie in the basket. 8. Air fry at 175 °C for 10 to 15 minutes, or until the pastry is golden brown and cooked through.
Per Serving: Calories 598; Fat 48.02g; Sodium 1075mg; Carbs 5.6g; Fibre 0.6g; Sugar 4g; Protein 36.13g

Italian Toasted Ravioli

Prep Time: 15 minutes| **Cook Time:** 10 minutes| **Serves:** 6

2 large eggs
2 tablespoons milk
30 g plain flour
80 g Italian bread crumbs
35 g grated Parmesan cheese
1 teaspoon Italian seasoning
¼ teaspoon salt
¼ teaspoon freshly ground black pepper
1 (200 g) package fresh ravioli, refrigerated
Extra-virgin olive oil, for spraying
Marinara sauce, for serving (optional)

1. To prepare, heat your air fryer to 195 °C. 2. Pour the milk in a small shallow bowl and whisk together with 2 eggs. Put the flour in a second small shallow bowl. Combine the bread crumbs, Parmesan cheese, Italian seasoning, salt, and pepper in a third small shallow bowl. 3. Coat each ravioli in the flour, in the egg wash, and then in the bread crumb mixture. 4. Lightly spritz the air fryer basket with oil, putting the ravioli in a single layer in the basket and lightly spraying with oil. 5. Air fry at 175 °C for 4 minutes. 6. Flip the ravioli and lightly spray with oil. 7. Air fry for another 3 to 4 minutes, or until golden brown and crispy. 8. Serve it with marinara sauce, if using.
Per Serving: Calories 119; Fat 4.88g; Sodium 381mg; Carbs 13.43g; Fibre 1g; Sugar 1.46g; Protein 4.98g

Baked Jalapeño Poppers

Prep Time: 15 minutes| **Cook Time:** 10 minutes| **Serves:** 8

8 large jalapeños
200 g cream cheese, at room temperature
55 g panko bread crumbs
50 g shredded cheese, any variety
2 teaspoons dried parsley
½ teaspoon garlic powder
Extra-virgin olive oil, for the basket

1. Preheat the air fryer to 185 °C. 2. Remove the stems of the jalapeños, and then cut them in half lengthwise. 3. Carefully remove the seeds and insides to create boats. 4. Combine the cream cheese, bread crumbs, shredded cheese, parsley, and garlic powder in a medium bowl. 5. Stuff each jalapeño half with the cream cheese mixture. 6. Lightly spritz the air fryer basket with the extra-virgin olive oil, placing the poppers in a single layer in the basket. 7. Air fry at 185 °C for 7 to 10 minutes, or until the cheese is bubbly and golden brown and the jalapeños have softened.
Per Serving: Calories 126; Fat 11.15g; Sodium 216mg; Carbs 2.57g; Fibre 0.2g; Sugar 1.17g; Protein 4.31g

Cheese Pizza Pinwheels

Prep Time: 10 minutes| **Cook Time:** 20 minutes| **Serves:** 4

1 tablespoon flour
1 (200 g) can crescent dough, refrigerated
125 g pizza sauce
55 g mozzarella cheese
50 g shredded Parmesan cheese
Extra-virgin olive oil, for the basket

1. Preheat the air fryer to 175 °C. 2. Lightly coat your work surface with flour, then roll out the sheet of crescent dough. 3. Add the pizza sauce evenly over the crescent dough all the way to the edges. 4. Sprinkle the mozzarella cheese and Parmesan cheese over top of the pizza sauce. 5. Roll up the dough into a long tube. 6. Place the rolled tube in the freezer for about 10 minutes to make cutting easier. 7. Cut the dough roll into 2.5 cm slices. 8. Lightly spray the air fryer basket with oil. 9. Place the pinwheel slices in a single layer in the basket. 10. Allow about 1 cm between each. 11. Air fry at 175 °C for 5 minutes. 12. Shake the basket and air fry for another 2 to 5 minutes, or until golden brown and cooked through.
Per Serving: Calories 111; Fat 4.15g; Sodium 463mg; Carbs 8.95g; Fibre 1g; Sugar 1.42g; Protein 9.26g

Garlic Buffalo Chicken Meatballs

Prep Time: 10 minutes| **Cook Time:** 15 minutes| **Serves:** 4

455 g chicken mince
55 g panko bread crumbs
1 large egg
3 tablespoons buffalo sauce, divided
2 teaspoons minced garlic
1 teaspoon dry ranch dressing mix
½ teaspoon salt
½ teaspoon freshly ground black pepper
Extra-virgin olive oil, for the basket

1. To prepare. heat the air fryer to 175 °C. 2. Combine the chicken, bread crumbs, egg, 1 tablespoon buffalo sauce, garlic, ranch dressing mix, salt, and pepper in a large bowl. 3. Form the mixture into 2.5 cm meatballs, and make sure it has about 20 meatballs. 4. Lightly spray the air fryer basket with oil, and place the meatballs in a single layer in the basket. (Air fry in batches, if necessary.) 5. Air fry at 175 °C for 6 minutes. 6. Then shake the basket and air fry again for another 6 to 9 minutes, or until browned and cooked through. 7. Toss with the remaining 2 tablespoons buffalo sauce before serving.
Per Serving: Calories 280; Fat 18.94g; Sodium 500mg; Carbs 3.76g; Fibre 0.4g; Sugar 0.88g; Protein 22.47g

Loaded Potato Skins with Black Pepper

Prep Time: 10 minutes| **Cook Time:** 60 minutes| **Serves:** 6

Extra-virgin olive oil, for greasing the basket
6 medium russet potatoes, scrubbed
Salt
Freshly ground black pepper
6 slices cooked bacon, crumbled
100 g shredded cheddar cheese
115g sour cream, for serving
3 spring onions, thinly sliced, for serving

1. To prepare, heat the air fryer to 205 °C. 2. Lightly spray the air fryer basket with oil. Lightly spritz the potatoes with oil and season with salt and pepper. Pierce each potato a few times with a fork. 3. Place the potatoes in the basket. Air fry at 205 °C for 30 to 40 minutes, until fork-tender. 4. Set aside the potatoes for 5 to 10 minutes, or until cool enough to handle. 5. Cut the potatoes in half lengthwise. Scoop out most of the insides, leaving about ½ cm so the potato skins hold their shape and resemble a boat. 6. Season the inside of the potato skins with salt and pepper. 7. Lightly spray with oil. 8. Spread the potato skins evenly in a single layer in the basket, leaving about ½ cm of space between each to ensure even cooking. (Air fry in batches, if necessary.) Air fry the potato skins for 8 to 10 minutes, until crispy and golden. 9. Carefully sprinkle the bacon and cheese into each potato skin. 10. Air fry for an additional 2 to 3 minutes, or until the cheese is melted and bubbly. 11. Top with sour cream and spring onions before serving.
Per Serving: Calories 423; Fat 5.37g; Sodium 157mg; Carbs 68.25g; Fibre 4.8g; Sugar 2.55; Protein 11.83g

Air-fryer Egg Rolls

Prep Time: 15 minutes| **Cook Time:** 10 minutes| **Serves:** 5

1 (375 g) can black beans, drained and rinsed
165 g corn kernels, frozen or canned, drained
1 (100 g) can diced green chiles
195 g shredded Colby-Jack cheese
1 teaspoon paprika
1 teaspoon chili powder
1 teaspoon salt
½ teaspoon ground cumin
½ teaspoon freshly ground black pepper
1 (300 g) package egg roll wrappers
Extra-virgin olive oil, for spraying

1. To prepare, heat the air fryer to 190 °C. 2. Combine the black beans, corn, green chiles, cheese, paprika, chili powder, salt, cumin, and pepper in a large bowl. 3. Place an egg roll wrapper on your work surface diagonally. 4. Put some filling onto the centre of the wrapper. 5. Fold the bottom corner over the filling and roll up snugly halfway to cover the filling. 6. Fold in both sides of the wrapper. 7. Moisten the edges of the top corner with water, roll up the rest of the way, and seal the top corner. 8. Repeat steps 2 and 3 with the remaining ingredients. 9. Lightly spray the air fryer basket with oil. 10. Place the egg rolls seam-side down in the basket, leaving at least ½ cm between each to ensure even cooking. 11. Lightly spray with oil. 12. Air fry at 190 °C for 4 minutes. 13. Flip the egg rolls and lightly spray with oil. 14. Air fry the egg rolls for another 4 to 6 minutes, or until golden brown and crispy.
Per Serving: Calories 269; Fat 18.02g; Sodium 963mg; Carbs 13.66g; Fibre 2.7g; Sugar 1.61g; Protein 15.07g

Fried Edamame

Prep Time: 5 minutes| **Cook Time:** 10 minutes| **Serves:** 4

Olive oil
1 (400 g) bag frozen edamame in pods
½ teaspoon salt
½ teaspoon garlic salt
¼ teaspoon freshly ground black pepper
½ teaspoon red pepper flakes (optional)

1.Spray an air fryer basket lightly with olive oil. 2. Add the frozen edamame in a medium bowl, lightly spray with olive oil, and toss to coat. 3. Mix together the salt, garlic salt, black pepper, and red pepper flakes (if using) in a small bowl. 4. Add the mixture to the edamame and toss until evenly coated. 5. Place half the edamame in the fryer basket, and make sure it won't be overfilled the basket. 6. Air fry at 190 °C for 5 minutes. 7. Shake the basket and cook until the edamame is starting to brown and get crispy, 3 to 5 more minutes. 8. Repeat with the remaining edamame and serve immediately.
Per Serving: Calories 97; Fat 4.04g; Sodium 296mg; Carbs 33.42g; Fibre 4.1g; Sugar 1.98g; Protein 8.57g

Spicy Fried Chickpeas

Prep Time: 5 minutes| **Cook Time:** 20 minutes| **Serves:** 4

Olive oil
½ teaspoon ground cumin
½ teaspoon chili powder
¼ teaspoon cayenne pepper
¼ teaspoon salt
1 (475 g) can chickpeas, drained and rinsed

1. Spray a fryer basket lightly with olive oil. 2. Combine the cumin, chili powder, cayenne pepper, and salt in a small bowl. 3. Add the chickpeas in a medium bowl and lightly spray them with olive oil. 4. Add the spice mixture and toss until coated evenly. 5. Transfer the chickpeas to the fryer basket. 6. Air fry at 200 °C until the chickpeas reach your desired level of crunchiness, for 15 to 20 minutes, making sure to shake the basket every 5 minutes.
Per Serving: Calories 90; Fat 1.7g; Sodium 290mg; Carbs 14.89g; Fibre 4.2g; Sugar 2.58g; Protein 4.58g

Spicy Onion Rings

Prep Time: 15 minutes| **Cook Time:** 10 minutes| **Serves:** 6

2 large sweet onions
125 g plain flour
1 teaspoon baking powder
2 teaspoons salt, divided
2 large eggs
2 tablespoons milk
215 g panko bread crumbs
1 teaspoon smoked paprika
½ teaspoon onion powder
½ teaspoon garlic powder
½ teaspoon freshly ground black pepper
Pinch cayenne pepper
Extra-virgin olive oil, for spraying

1. Cut the ends of the onions off, peel off the skins, slice into ½ cm-thick rings, and separate the rings. 2. Combine the flour, baking powder, and 1 teaspoon salt in a small shallow bowl. 3. Whisk together the eggs and milk in a second small shallow bowl. 4. Combine the bread crumbs, paprika, onion powder, garlic powder, black pepper, and cayenne pepper in a third small shallow bowl. 5. Preheat the air fryer to 195 °C. 6. Coat the onions in the flour mixture, then in the egg mixture, and then in the bread crumbs. 7. Press on the bread crumbs to ensure they adhere. 8. Lightly spray the air fryer basket with oil, placing the onion rings in a single layer in the basket and lightly spraying with oil. 9. Air fry at 175 °C for 5 minutes. 10. Gently flip the onion rings and lightly spray with oil. 11. Air fry the onion rings for another 5 minutes, or until golden brown and crispy.
Per Serving: Calories 166; Fat 2.4g; Sodium 847mg; Carbs 31g; Fibre 2.1g; Sugar 6.6g; Protein 5.24g

Fried Black Bean Corn Dip

Prep Time: 10 minutes| **Cook Time:** 10 minutes| **Serves:** 4

½ (375 g) can black beans, drained and rinsed
½ (375 g) can corn, drained and rinsed
70 g chunky salsa
50 g reduced-fat cream cheese, softened
25 g shredded reduced-fat Cheddar cheese
½ teaspoon ground cumin
½ teaspoon paprika
Salt
Freshly ground black pepper

1. Mix together the black beans, corn, salsa, cream cheese, Cheddar cheese, cumin, and paprika in a medium bowl. 2. Add salt and the freshly ground black pepper to season the mixture and stir until well combined. 3. Spoon the mixture into an air fryer–safe baking dish. 4. Place baking dish in the fryer basket and air fry at 160 °C until heated through, for about 10 minutes. 5. Serve hot.
Per Serving: Calories 105; Fat 4.98g; Sodium 427mg; Carbs 12.86g; Fibre 1.4g; Sugar 3.52g; Protein 4.16g

Crunchy Tortilla Chips

Prep Time: 5 minutes| **Cook Time:** 5 minutes| **Serves:** 4

Olive oil
½ teaspoon salt
½ teaspoon ground cumin
½ teaspoon chili powder
½ teaspoon paprika
Pinch cayenne pepper
8 (15 cm) corn tortillas, each cut into 6 wedges

1. Spray fryer basket lightly with olive oil. 2. Combine the salt, cumin, chili powder, paprika, and cayenne pepper in a small bowl. 3. Place the tortilla wedges in the fryer basket in a single layer. 4. Spray the tortillas lightly with oil and sprinkle with some of the seasoning mixture. 5. Cook the tortillas in batches. 6. Air fry at 190 °C for 2 to 3 minutes. 7. Shake the basket and cook until the chips are light brown and crispy, an additional 2 to 3 minutes. Watch the chips closely to avoid burning.
Per Serving: Calories 3; Fat 0.15g; Sodium 301mg; Carbs 0.46g; Fibre 0.3g; Sugar 0.06g; Protein 0.14g

Spicy and Sweet Chicken Wings

Prep Time: 10 minutes| **Cook Time:** 15 minutes| **Serves:** 6

For the wings
900 g fresh bone-in chicken wings
1 tablespoon baking powder
2 teaspoons salt
Extra-virgin olive oil, for spraying
For the sauce
8 tablespoons butter, melted
1 tablespoon lemon-pepper seasoning
2 teaspoons honey

To make the wings: 1. To prepare, heat your air fryer to 205 °C. 2. Pat the chicken wings dry with paper towels. 3. Mix together the baking powder and salt in a large zip-top bag. 4. Add the chicken wings, seal the bag, and shake to coat evenly. 5. Lightly spray the air fryer basket with oil. 6. Arrange evenly the chicken wings in a single layer in the basket (Air fry in batches, if necessary.), and lightly spray with oil again. 7. Air fry at   175 °C for 7 minutes, and then flip the wings and lightly spray with oil. 8. Air fry for another 6 to 8 minutes, or until the wings are crispy and lightly browned and have reached an internal temperature of 75 °C.
To make the sauce: While the wings are air frying, whisk together the melted butter, lemon-pepper seasoning, and honey in a small bowl.
As soon as the wings are done, toss them in the lemon-pepper sauce to coat.
Per Serving: Calories 333; Fat 20.71g; Sodium 1019mg; Carbs 1.95g; Fibre 0g; Sugar 1.94g; Protein 33.39g

Simple Crab Rangoon

Prep Time: 15 minutes| **Cook Time:** 10 minutes| **Serves:** 6

200 g cream cheese, at room temperature
1 (150 g) white crabmeat, picked through and drained
1 teaspoon minced garlic
½ teaspoon soy sauce
½ teaspoon icing sugar
½ teaspoon dried chives
1 (300 – 400 g) package wonton wrappers
Extra-virgin olive oil, for spraying

1. To prepare, heat the air fryer to 175 °C. 2. Mix together the cream cheese, crabmeat, garlic, soy sauce, icing sugar, and chives in a medium bowl. 3. Lay out the wonton wrappers and place a heaping teaspoon of cream cheese in the centre of each. 4. Dab a bit of water on the outer edges of the wrappers and fold the two ends together to form a small pocket. Pinch the edges tightly to seal. 5. Lightly spritz the air fryer basket with oil. 6. Place the crab rangoon in a single layer in the basket. 7. Lightly spray with oil. Air fry at 175 °C for 7 minutes, or until golden brown and crispy.
Per Serving: Calories 131; Fat 10.98g; Sodium 202mg; Carbs 4.99g; Fibre 0.1g; Sugar 1.69g; Protein 3.36g

Simple Fried Pickles

Prep Time: 15 minutes| **Cook Time:** 15 minutes| **Serves:** 4

125 g plain flour
1 teaspoon paprika
1 large egg
140 g panko bread crumbs
1 (600 g) jar dill pickle spears
Extra-virgin olive oil, for spraying

1. Preheat the air fryer to 205 °C. 2. Combine the flour and paprika in a small shallow bowl. Whisk the egg in a second small shallow bowl. Put the bread crumbs in a third small shallow bowl. 3. Pat the pickle spears dry with paper towels. 4. Coat each pickle spear in the flour mixture, then in the egg, and then in the bread crumbs. 5. Lightly spray the air fryer basket with oil. 6. Place the pickle spears in a single layer in the basket, leaving about ½ cm of space between each to ensure even cooking. (Air fry in batches, if necessary.) 7. Lightly spray with oil. Air fry at 205 °C for 7 minutes. 8. Gently flip the pickles and air fry for an additional 5 to 8 minutes, or until lightly browned and crispy.
Per Serving: Calories 131; Fat 10.98g; Sodium 202mg; Carbs 4.99g; Fibre 0.1g; Sugar 1.69g; Protein 3.36g

Air-fryer Parmesan-Asparagus Twists

Prep Time: 15 minutes| **Cook Time:** 15 minutes| **Serves:** 6

24 asparagus spears
1 tablespoon extra-virgin olive oil, plus more for the basket
¼ teaspoon salt
¼ teaspoon freshly ground black pepper
Flour, for dusting
1 sheet puff pastry, at room temperature
1 large egg
1 teaspoon water
50 g grated Parmesan cheese
¼ teaspoon cayenne pepper

1. Combine the asparagus, olive oil, salt, and black pepper in a large bowl, and toss to coat.   2. Preheat the air fryer to 175 °C. 3. Dust your work surface with flour, then unfold the puff pastry sheet. 4. Cut the sheet in half lengthwise, then cut each half into thin strips about 1 cm. 5. wide, and make it sure it will have 24 strips. 6. Wrap a pastry strip around each asparagus spear, leaving the tip free. 7. Place the wrapped spears on a baking sheet. 8. Whisk together the egg and water in a small shallow bowl. 9. Combine the Parmesan cheese and cayenne pepper in a second small shallow bowl. 10. Brush each wrapped spear with the egg wash, then sprinkle with the cheese mixture. 11. Press on the mixture to ensure it adheres. 12. Lightly spray the air fryer basket with oil, and place the twists in a single layer in the basket, leaving about 1 cm of space between each. (Air fry in batches, if necessary.) 13. Air fry at 175 °C for 10 minutes, shaking the basket once while cooking, until the pastry is lightly browned.
Per Serving: Calories 67; Fat 5.37g; Sodium 249mg; Carbs 1.85g; Fibre 0.3g; Sugar 0.29g; Protein 3.14g

Italian Stuffed Mushroom Caps

Prep Time: 15 minutes| **Cook Time:** 10 minutes| **Serves:** 5

24 large cremini mushrooms
100 g cream cheese, at room temperature
55 g shredded mozzarella cheese
50 g grated Parmesan cheese
30 g Italian seasoned bread crumbs
1 large egg
¼ teaspoon salt
¼ teaspoon freshly ground black pepper
¼ teaspoon onion powder
Dash hot sauce
Extra-virgin olive oil, for spraying

1. Clean the mushrooms gently with a damp paper towel and remove the stems. 2. Use an electric mixer to combine the cream cheese, mozzarella cheese, Parmesan cheese, bread crumbs, egg, salt, pepper, onion powder, and hot sauce in a medium bowl. 3. Preheat the air fryer to 185 °C. 4. Spoon the cheese mixture into each mushroom, pressing the mixture into the mushrooms and leaving a little bit mounded over the top. 5. Lightly spray the air fryer basket with oil. 6. Place the stuffed mushrooms in a single layer in the basket. (Air fry in batches, if necessary.), and lightly spray with oil. Air fry at 185 °C for 7 to 10 minutes, or until both the mushrooms and the cheese have started to brown lightly on top.
Per Serving: Calories 144; Fat 9.22g; Sodium 405mg; Carbs 6.57g; Fibre 1.4g; Sugar 3.28; Protein 10.73g

Simple Bacon-Wrapped Jumbo Prawn

Prep Time: 10 minutes| **Cook Time:** 15 minutes| **Serves:** 6

455 g sliced bacon
400 g jumbo prawns, peeled and deveined, tails on
Extra-virgin olive oil, for the basket

1. Preheat the fryer to 190 °C. 2. Cut the bacon strips in half. Wrap half a strip tightly around each prawn. 3. Spritz the air fryer basket lightly with oil. 4. Place each bacon-wrapped prawn seam-side down in the basket. Air fry at 190 °C for 12 to 15 minutes, or until the bacon is crispy and cooked to your preference. 5. Check the progress after about 6 minutes and move the prawns around a little so they don't stick to the basket.
Per Serving: Calories 383; Fat 30.72g; Sodium 1013mg; Carbs 0.63g; Fibre 0g; Sugar 0.63; Protein 24.91g

Courgette Chips

Prep Time: 10 minutes| **Cook Time:** 15 minutes| **Serves:** 4

Olive oil
2 large courgettes, cut into ¼ cm-thick slices
2 teaspoons Cajun seasoning

1. Spray a fryer basket lightly with olive oil. 2. Put the courgette slices in a medium bowl and spray them generously with olive oil. 3. Sprinkle the Cajun seasoning over the courgette and stir to make sure they are evenly coated with oil and seasoning. 4. Place slices in a single layer in the fryer basket, making sure not to overcrowd but cook these in several batches. 5. Air fry at 185 °C for 8 minutes. 6. Flip the slices over and air fry until they are as crisp and brown as you prefer, for an additional 7 to 8 minutes.
Per Serving: Calories 6; Fat 0.03g; Sodium 103mg; Carbs 1.08g; Fibre 0.3g; Sugar 0.15g; Protein 0.28g

Mexican Fried Potato Skins

Prep Time: 10 minutes| **Cook Time:** 55 minutes| **Serves:** 6

Olive oil
6 medium russet potatoes, scrubbed
Salt
Freshly ground black pepper
230 g fat-free refried black beans
1 tablespoon taco seasoning
145 g salsa
75 g reduced-fat shredded Cheddar cheese

1. Lightly spray an air fryer basket with olive oil. 2. Spritz the potatoes lightly with oil and season with salt and pepper. 3. Pierce each potato a few times with a fork. 4. Place the potatoes in the air fryer basket, and air fry at 205 °C until fork tender, for 30 to 40 minutes. 5. Meanwhile, mix together the beans and taco seasoning in a small bowl. 6. Set them aside until the potatoes are cool enough to handle. 7. Cut each potato in half lengthwise. 8. Then scoop out most of the insides, leaving about ½ cm in the skins so the potato skins hold their shape. 9. Season the insides of the potato skins with salt and black pepper. 10. Lightly spritz the insides of the potato skins with oil, and cook them in batches. 11. Place them into the air fryer basket, skin side down, and air fry until crisp and golden, for 8 to 10 minutes. 12. Transfer the potato skins to a work surface and spoon ½ tablespoon of seasoned refried black beans into each one. 13. Top each with 2 teaspoons salsa and 1 tablespoon shredded Cheddar cheese. 14. Place filled potato skins in the air fryer basket in a single layer, and lightly spray with oil. 15. Air fry them until the cheese is melted and bubbly, for 2 to 3 minutes.
Per Serving: Calories 361; Fat 1.66g; Sodium 587mg; Carbs 74.48g; Fibre 7.2g; Sugar 3.62g; Protein 14.37g

Crispy Chicken Wings

Prep Time: 10 minutes| **Cook Time:** 15 minutes| **Serves:** 4

Olive oil
2 tablespoons Old Bay seasoning
2 teaspoons baking powder
2 teaspoons salt
900 g chicken wings, pat dry with paper towel

1. Spray an air fryer basket lightly with olive oil. 2. Mix together the Old Bay seasoning, baking powder, and salt in a large zip-top plastic bag. 3. Place the wings in the zip-top bag, seal, and toss with the seasoning mixture until evenly coated.   4. Place the seasoned wings in the air fryer basket in a single layer. 5. Lightly spray with olive oil, and cook them in batches. 6. Air fry at 205 °C for 7 minutes. 7. Turn the wings over, lightly spray them with olive oil, and air fry until the wings are crispy and lightly browned, for 5 to 8 more minutes. 8. Using a meat thermometer, check to make sure the internal temperature is 75 °C or higher.
Per Serving: Calories 289; Fat 8.1g; Sodium 1347mg; Carbs 0.67g; Fibre 0.2g; Sugar 0g; Protein 49.9g

Prosciutto-Wrapped Asparagus

Prep Time: 10 minutes| **Cook Time:** 10 minutes| **Serves:** 4

450 g asparagus
12 (15 g) slices prosciutto
1 tablespoon coconut oil, melted
2 teaspoons lemon juice
⅛ teaspoon red pepper flakes
35 g grated Parmesan cheese
2 tablespoons salted butter, melted

1. Place an asparagus spear onto a slice of prosciutto on a clean work surface. 2. Drizzle with coconut oil and lemon juice. 3. Sprinkle it with red pepper flakes and Parmesan across asparagus. 4. Roll prosciutto around asparagus spear. 5. Place them into the air fryer basket. 6. Adjust the temperature to 190 °C and set the timer for 10 minutes. 7. Drizzle the asparagus roll with butter before serving.
Per Serving: Calories 201; Fat 14.3g; Sodium 481mg; Carbs 7.7g; Fibre 2.4g; Sugar 3.2g; Protein 12.4g

Fried Bacon-Wrapped Jalapeño Poppers

Prep Time: 15 minutes| **Cook Time:** 12 minutes| **Serves:** 4

6 jalapeños (about 10 cm long each)
75 g full-fat cream cheese
35 g shredded medium Cheddar cheese
¼ teaspoon garlic powder
12 slices bacon

1. Cut the tops off of the jalapeños and slice down the centre lengthwise into two pieces. 2. Use a knife to carefully remove white membrane and seeds from peppers. 3. Place cream cheese, Cheddar, and garlic powder in a large microwave-safe bowl. 4. Microwave for 30 seconds and stir it. 5. Spoon cheese mixture into hollow jalapeños. 6. Wrap a slice of bacon around each jalapeño half, completely covering pepper. 7. Place it into the air fryer basket. 8. Adjust the temperature to 205 °C and set the timer for 12 minutes. 9. Turn the peppers halfway through the cooking time. 10. Serve it warm.
Per Serving: Calories 405; Fat 37g; Sodium 504mg; Carbs 4g; Fibre 0g; Sugar 2.8g; Protein 14g

Almond and Mozzarella Cheese Pizza Rolls

Prep Time: 15 minutes| **Cook Time:** 10 minutes| **Serves:** 8

225 g shredded mozzarella cheese
50 g almond flour
2 large eggs
72 slices pepperoni
8 (25 g) mozzarella string cheese sticks, cut into 3 pieces each
2 tablespoons unsalted butter, melted
¼ teaspoon garlic powder
½ teaspoon dried parsley
2 tablespoons grated Parmesan cheese

1. Place mozzarella and almond flour in a large microwave-safe bowl. Microwave it for 1 minute. 2. Remove bowl and mix it until ball of dough forms. Microwave it additional 30 seconds if necessary. 3. Crack eggs into the bowl and mix them until smooth dough ball forms. 4. Get your hands wet with water and knead the dough briefly. Use nonstick cooking spray to spray one side of each with nonstick cooking spray. 5. Place the dough ball between the two sheets of parchment paper, with sprayed sides facing dough. 6. Roll dough out to ½ cm thickness. Use a knife to slice into 24 rectangles. 7. Place 3 pepperoni slices and 1 piece string cheese on each rectangle. 8. Fold the rectangle in half, covering pepperoni and cheese filling. Pinch or roll sides closed. 9. Cut a piece of parchment to fit your air fryer basket and place it into the basket. 10. Put the rolls onto the parchment. Adjust the temperature setting to 175 °C and set the timer for 10 minutes. 11. Open the air fryer and flip the pizza rolls after 5 minutes. Restart the air fryer and continue cooking until pizza rolls are golden. 12. Place butter, garlic powder, and parsley in a small bowl. Brush the mixture over cooked pizza rolls and then sprinkle it with Parmesan. 13. Serve warm.
Per Serving: Calories 166; Fat 11.27g; Sodium 553mg; Carbs 1.41g; Fibre 0.5g; Sugar 0.45g; Protein 14.26g

Fried Parmesan Chicken Wings

Prep Time: 5 minutes| **Cook Time:** 25 minutes| **Serves:** 4

900 g raw chicken wings
1 teaspoon pink Himalayan salt
½ teaspoon garlic powder
1 tablespoon baking powder
4 tablespoons unsalted butter, melted
35 g grated Parmesan cheese
¼ teaspoon dried parsley

1. Place chicken wings, salt, ½ teaspoon garlic powder, and baking powder in a large bowl, and then toss it. 2. Place wings into the air fryer basket. 3. Adjust the temperature to 205 °C and set the timer for 25 minutes. 4. Then toss the basket several times during the cooking time. 5. Combine butter, Parmesan, and parsley in a small bowl. 6. Remove wings from the air fryer and place them into a clean large bowl. 7. Pour the butter mixture over the wings and toss it until coated. 6. Serve it warm.
Per Serving: Calories 393; Fat 18.05g; Sodium 338mg; Carbs 1.69g; Fibre 0.1g; Sugar 0.02g; Protein 57.3g

Bacon Jalapeño Cheese Bread

Prep Time: 10 minutes| **Cook Time:** 15 minutes| **Serves:** 4

225 g shredded mozzarella cheese
25 g grated Parmesan cheese
65 g chopped pickled jalapeños
2 large eggs
4 slices bacon, cooked and chopped

1. Mix all ingredients in a large bowl. 2. Cut a piece of parchment to fit your air fryer basket. 3. Dampen your hands with a bit of water and press out the mixture into a circle. 4. Separate this into two smaller cheese breads, depending on the size of your air fryer. 5. Place the parchment and cheese bread into the air fryer basket. 5. Adjust the temperature to 160 °C and set the timer for 15 minutes. 6. Carefully flip the bread when 5 minutes remain. 7. When fully cooked, the top will be golden brown. 8. Serve it warm.
Per Serving: Calories 237; Fat 12.71g; Sodium 868mg; Carbs 6.69g; Fibre 1.1g; Sugar 3.21g; Protein 24.07g

Bacon Cheeseburger Dip

Prep Time: 20 minutes| **Cook Time:** 10 minutes| **Serves:** 6

200 g full-fat cream cheese
55 g full-fat mayonnaise
55 g full-fat sour cream
40 g chopped onion
1 teaspoon garlic powder
1 tablespoon Worcestershire sauce
125 g shredded medium Cheddar cheese, divided
225 g cooked lean beef mince
6 slices bacon, cooked and crumbled
2 large pickle spears, chopped

1. Add cream cheese in a large microwave-safe bowl and microwave it for 45 seconds. 2. Stir it with mayonnaise, sour cream, onion, garlic powder, Worcestershire sauce, and 100 g Cheddar. 3. Add cooked beef mince and bacon. 4. Sprinkle remaining Cheddar on top. 5. Place it in 6 bowls and put them into the air fryer basket. 6. Adjust the temperature setting to 205 °C and set the timer for 10 minutes. 7. Dip it when top is golden and bubbling. 8. Sprinkle pickles over dish. 9. Serve it warm.
Per Serving: Calories 231; Fat 14.24g; Sodium 473mg; Carbs 7.57g; Fibre 0.6g; Sugar 3.12g; Protein 17.63g

Mozzarella Cheese Sticks

Prep Time: 60 minutes| **Cook Time:** 10 minutes| **Serves:** 4

6 (25 g) mozzarella string cheese sticks
50 g grated Parmesan cheese
1 teaspoon dried parsley
2 large eggs

1. Place mozzarella sticks on a cutting board and cut it in half. 2. Freeze it for 45 minutes until it's firm, or remove frozen sticks after 1 hour if freezing overnight, and place into airtight zip-top storage bag and put back in freezer for future use. 3. Mix Parmesan and parsley in a large bowl. 4. Whisk eggs in a medium bowl. 5. Dip a frozen mozzarella stick into beaten eggs and then into Parmesan mixture to coat. 6. Repeat with remaining sticks. 7. Place mozzarella sticks into the air fryer basket. 8. Adjust the temperature setting to 205 °C and set the timer for 10 minutes or until it's golden. 9. Serve it warm.
Per Serving: Calories 87; Fat 5.99g; Sodium 233mg; Carbs 2.06g; Fibre 0g; Sugar 0.06g; Protein 5.99g

Bacon-Wrapped Onion Rings

Prep Time: 5 minutes| **Cook Time:** 10 minutes| **Serves:** 4

1 large onion, peeled
1 tablespoon sriracha
8 slices bacon

1. Slice onion into ½ cm thick slices. 2. Brush sriracha over the onion slices. 3. Take two slices of onion and wrap bacon around the rings. 4. Repeat with remaining onion and bacon. 5. Place it into the air fryer basket. 6. Adjust the temperature to 175 °C and set the timer for 10 minutes. 7. Use tongs to flip the onion rings halfway through the cooking time. 8. Serve it warm.
Per Serving: Calories 105; Fat 0.04g; Sodium 2mg; Carbs 3.5g; Fibre 0.6g; Sugar 2g; Protein 7g

Spinach Artichoke Dip

Prep Time: 10 minutes| **Cook Time:** 10 minutes| **Serves:** 6

250 g frozen spinach, drained and thawed
1 (350 g) can artichoke hearts, drained and chopped
65 g chopped pickled jalapeños
200 g full-fat cream cheese, softened
55 g full-fat mayonnaise
55 g full-fat sour cream
½ teaspoon garlic powder
25 g grated Parmesan cheese
105 g shredded pepper jack cheese

1. Mix all ingredients in baking bowl. Place it into the air fryer basket. 2. Adjust the temperature to 160 °C and set the timer for 10 minutes. 3. Remove it when brown and bubbling. 4. Serve it warm.
Per Serving: Calories 255; Fat 17.49g; Sodium 498mg; Carbs 13.82g; Fibre 3.9g; Sugar 4.6g; Protein 12.81g

Simple Mozzarella Pizza Crust

Prep Time: 5 minutes| **Cook Time:** 10 minutes| **Serves:** 1

55 g shredded whole-milk mozzarella cheese
2 tablespoons blanched finely ground almond flour
1 tablespoon full-fat cream cheese
1 large egg white

1. Place cream cheese, mozzarella, and almond flour, and cream cheese in a medium microwave-safe bowl. Microwave it for 30 seconds. 2. Stir them until smooth ball of dough forms. 3. Add egg white and stir them until soft round dough forms. 4. Press into a 6 round pizza crust. Cut a piece of parchment to fit your air fryer basket and place crust on the parchment. 5. Put it into the air fryer basket. Adjust the temperature setting to 175 °C and set the timer for 10 minutes. 6. Flip it after 5 minutes and place any desired toppings on the crust. 7. Continue cooking until it's golden. 8. Serve it immediately.
Per Serving: Calories 323; Fat 24.42g; Sodium 463mg; Carbs 6.08g; Fibre 1.8g; Sugar 2.53g; Protein 21.08g

Fresh and Bright Orange Cheesecake

Prep Time: 10 minutes | **Cook Time:** 19 minutes | **Serves:** 8

300 g cream cheese, at room temperature
2 tablespoons sour cream
2 large eggs
10 g granular sweetener
1 tablespoon fresh orange zest
1 tablespoon fresh orange juice
1 teaspoon vanilla extract
⅛ teaspoon salt

1. In a medium bowl, combine cream cheese, sour cream, eggs, sweetener, orange zest, orange juice, vanilla, and salt until smooth. Spoon into an ungreased 23 cm spring-form pan. Cover with aluminum foil. 2. Preheat air fryer at 205 °C for 3 minutes. 3. Place spring-form pan into air fryer basket and cook 14 minutes. 4. Reduce the cooking temperature to 175 °C, remove aluminum foil, and cook an additional 5 minutes. 5. The cheesecake will be a little jiggly in the centre, cover it and refrigerate a minimum of 2 hours to allow it to set. Release sides from pan.
Per Serving: Calories 189; Fat 16.48g; Sodium 469mg; Carbs 3.01g; Fibre 0g; Sugar 1.91g; Protein7.76 g

Delicious Candied Walnuts

Prep Time: 5 minutes | **Cook Time:** 16 minutes | **Serves:** 6

1 large egg white, beaten
¼ teaspoon vanilla extract
15 g brown sugar sweetener
¼ teaspoon ground cinnamon
⅛ teaspoon salt
350 g walnut halves

1. Preheat air fryer at 135 °C for 3 minutes. Lightly grease the air fryer basket with olive oil. 2. Whisk egg white together with vanilla, brown sugar, cinnamon, and salt in a bowl. Add walnuts and toss until well coated. 3. Place walnuts in air fryer basket, and cook them for 16 minutes, stirring them halfway through. 4. Let cool 10 minutes after cooking, then store in an airtight container at room temperature.
Per Serving: Calories 298; Fat 26.09g; Sodium 62mg; Carbs 13.96g; Fibre 2.7g; Sugar 9.26g; Protein 6.7 g

Gorgeous Marble Cheesecake

Prep Time: 10 minutes | **Cook Time:** 20 minutes | **Serves:** 8

60 g digestive biscuit crumbs
3 tablespoons butter, at room temperature
1½ (200 g) packages cream cheese, at room temperature
55 g sugar
2 eggs, beaten
1 tablespoon plain flour
1 teaspoon vanilla extract
75 g chocolate syrup

1. Stir the biscuit crumbs and butter in a bowl. Press the crust into the bottom of a 15-by-5-cm round baking pan and freeze to set while you prepare the filling. 2. Stir together the cream cheese and sugar in a bowl until mixed well. 3. One at a time, beat in the eggs. Add the flour and vanilla and stir to combine. 4. Transfer ⅔ cup of filling to a small bowl and stir in the chocolate syrup until combined. 5. Insert the crisper plate into the air fryer basket, and preheat the air fryer at 160 °C for 3 minutes on Bake mode. 6. Pour the vanilla filling into the pan with the crust. Drop the chocolate filling over the vanilla filling by the spoonful. With a clean butter knife stir the fillings in a zigzag pattern to marbleize them. Do not let the knife touch the crust. 7. Once the unit is preheated, place the pan into the air fryer basket. 8. Bake the food at 160 °C for 20 minutes. 9. When the cooking is done, the cheesecake should be just set. Cool the dish on a wire rack for 1 hour. Refrigerate the cheesecake until firm before slicing.
Per Serving: Calories 214; Fat 15.62g; Sodium 206mg; Carbs 13.79g; Fibre 0.3g; Sugar 10.44g; Protein 4.84mg

Ultimate Chocolate Bread Pudding

Prep Time: 10 minutes | **Cook Time:** 10 minutes | **Serves:** 4

Nonstick baking spray
1 egg
1 egg yolk
180 ml chocolate milk
2 tablespoons cocoa powder
3 tablespoons light brown sugar
3 tablespoons peanut butter
1 teaspoon vanilla extract
5 slices firm white bread, cubed

1. Spray a 15-by-5-cm round baking pan with the baking spray. 2. In a medium bowl, whisk the egg, egg yolk, chocolate milk, cocoa powder, brown sugar, peanut butter, and vanilla until thoroughly combined. Stir in the bread cubes and let soak for 10 minutes. Spoon this mixture into the prepared pan. 3. Place the pan into the air fryer basket, and bake the food at 160 °C for 12 minutes. 4. Check the pudding after about 10 minutes. It is done when it is firm to the touch. If not, resume cooking. 5. When the cooking is complete, let the pudding cool for 5 minutes. 6. Serve warm.
Per Serving: Calories 277; Fat 7.45g; Sodium 239 mg; Carbs 43.73g; Fibre 4.7g; Sugar 10.83g; Protein 11.02g

Sweet Pineapple Cheese Wontons

Prep Time: 15 minutes | **Cook Time:** 15 minutes | **Serves:** 5

1 (200 g) package cream cheese
165 g finely chopped fresh pineapple
20 wonton wrappers
Cooking oil spray

1. Add the cream cheese to a small microwave-safe bowl, and heat the cream cheese in the microwave on high power for 20 seconds to soften. 2. Stir the cream cheese and pineapple until mixed well in a bowl. 3. Lay out the wonton wrappers on a work surface. 4. Spoon 1½ teaspoons of the cream cheese mixture onto each wrapper, do not to overfill. 5. Fold each wrapper diagonally across to form a triangle. Bring the 2 bottom corners up toward each other. Do not close the wrapper yet. Bring up the 2 open sides and push out any air. Squeeze the open edges together to seal. 6. Insert the crisper plate into the air fryer basket and the air fryer basket into the unit, and then preheat the air fryer at 200 °C for 3 minutes. 7. Once the unit is preheated, spray the crisper plate with cooking oil. 8. Place the wontons into the air fryer basket, and spray the wontons with the cooking oil. 8. Air Fry the wontons at 200 °C for 18 minutes. 9. After 10 minutes, remove the air fryer basket, flip each wonton, and spray them with more oil. Reinsert the air fryer basket to resume cooking for 5 to 8 minutes more until the wontons are light golden brown and crisp. 10. If cooking in batches, remove the cooked wontons from the air fryer basket and repeat steps 7, 8, and 9 for the remaining wontons. 11. When the cooking is complete, let the wontons cool for 5 minutes before serving.
Per Serving: Calories 552; Fat 16.59g; Sodium 942mg; Carbs 83.61g; Fibre 2.7g; Sugar 8.88g; Protein 16.16g

Sweet Blueberries Jubilee

Prep Time: 10 minutes | **Cook Time:** 9 minutes | **Serves:** 4

2 tablespoons butter, melted
5 g granular sweetener
2 teaspoons cream of tartar
1 tablespoon fresh orange juice
½ teaspoon orange zest
⅛ teaspoon ground cinnamon
⅛ teaspoon salt
295 g fresh blueberries

1. Preheat air fryer at 175 °C for 3 minutes. 2. Whisk together butter, sweetener, cream of tartar, orange juice, orange zest, cinnamon, and salt in a bowl. Toss in blueberries. Pour into an ungreased cake barrel. 3. Place cake barrel in air fryer basket, and cook for 9 minutes, stirring every 3 minutes. 4. Enjoy warmed or at room temperature.
Per Serving: Calories 112; Fat 4.59g; Sodium 82mg; Carbs 18.49g; Fibre 1.8g; Sugar 14.91g; Protein 0.889g

Irresistible Honey-Roasted Pears

Prep Time: 7 minutes | **Cook Time:** 25 minutes | **Serves:** 4

2 large pears, halved lengthwise and seeded
3 tablespoons honey
1 tablespoon unsalted butter
½ teaspoon ground cinnamon
30 g walnuts, chopped
60 g part-skim ricotta cheese, divided

1. Insert the crisper plate into the air fryer basket, and preheat the air fryer at 175 °C for 3 minutes on Air Roast mode. 2. In a 15-by-5-cm round pan, place the pears cut-side up. 3. In a small microwave-safe bowl, melt the honey, butter, and cinnamon. Brush this mixture over the cut sides of the pears. Pour 3 tablespoons of water around the pears in the pan. 4. Once the unit is preheated, place the pan into the air fryer basket. 5. Air Roast the food at 175 °C for 23 minutes. 6. After about 18 minutes, check the pears. They should be tender when pierced with a fork and slightly crisp on the edges. If not, resume cooking. 7. When the cooking is complete, baste the pears once with the liquid in the pan. Carefully remove the pears from the pan and place on a serving plate. Drizzle each with some liquid from the pan, sprinkle the walnuts on top, and serve with a spoonful of ricotta cheese.
Per Serving: Calories 194; Fat 6.52g; Sodium 18mg; Carbs 32.35g; Fibre 3.9g; Sugar 24.32g; Protein 3.1g

Delicious Baked Apples

Prep Time: 6 minutes | **Cook Time:** 20 minutes | **Serves:** 4

4 small Granny Smith apples
40 g chopped walnuts
55 g light brown sugar
2 tablespoons butter, melted
1 teaspoon ground cinnamon
½ teaspoon ground nutmeg
120 g water, or apple juice

1. Cut off the top third of the apples. Spoon out the core and some of the flesh and discard. Place the apples in a small air fryer baking pan. 2. Insert the crisper plate into the air fryer basket and the air fryer basket into the unit. Preheat the unit by selecting BAKE, setting the temperature to 175 °C, and setting the time to 3 minutes. Select START/STOP to begin. 3. Stir together the walnuts, brown sugar, melted butter, cinnamon, and nutmeg in a bowl. Spoon this mixture into the centres of the hollowed-out apples. 4. Once the unit is preheated, pour the water into the crisper plate. Place the baking pan into the air fryer basket. 5. Select BAKE, set the temperature to 175 °C, and set the time to 20 minutes. Select START/STOP to begin. 6. When the cooking is complete, the apples should be bubbly and fork-tender.
Per Serving: Calories 188; Fat 10.76g; Sodium 52mg; Carbs 22.08g; Fibre 4.9g; Sugar 14.28g; Protein 1.91g

Easy and Delicious Apple Fries

Prep Time: 10 minutes | **Cook Time:** 7 minutes | **Serves:** 8

Oil, for spraying
125 g plain flour
3 large eggs, beaten
60 g digestive biscuits
50 g sugar
1 teaspoon ground cinnamon
3 large Gala apples, peeled, cored, and cut into wedges
340 g caramel sauce, warmed

1. Turn on the air fryer and preheat it to 195 °C. Line the air fryer basket with parchment and sprinkle with oil. 2. Place the flour and beaten eggs in divide bowls and set aside. Mix together the digestive biscuit crumbs, sugar, and cinnamon in a bowl. 3. Working one at a time, coat the apple wedges in the flour, dip in the egg, and dredge in the digestive biscuit mix until evenly coated. 4. Place the apples in the air fryer basket, taking care not to overlap, and sprinkle with oil. 5. Cook for 5 minutes, flip, spray with oil, and cook for 2 more minutes. 6.Drizzle the caramel sauce over the top.
Per Serving: Calories 156; Fat 2.76g; Sodium242 mg; Carbs 29.43g; Fibre 3g; Sugar 12.67g; Protein 3.45g

Traditional Apple-Cinnamon Hand Pies

Prep Time: 15 minutes | Cook Time: 25 minutes | Serves: 8

2 apples, cored and diced
85 g honey
1 teaspoon ground cinnamon
1 teaspoon vanilla extract
⅛ teaspoon ground nutmeg
2 teaspoons cornflour
1 teaspoon water
4 refrigerated piecrusts
Cooking oil spray

1. Insert the crisper plate into the air fryer basket, and preheat the air fryer at 205 °C for 3 minutes. 2. Stir the apples, honey, cinnamon, vanilla, and nutmeg in a bowl. 3. Whisk the cornflour and water in a small bowl until the cornflour dissolves. 4. Once the unit is preheated, place the metal bowl with the apples into the air fryer basket. 5. Air Fry the apples at 205 °C for 5 minutes. 6. After 2 minutes, stir the apples. Resume cooking for 2 minutes. 7. Remove the bowl and stir the cornflour mixture into the apples. Reinsert the metal bowl into the air fryer basket and resume cooking for about 30 seconds until the sauce thickens slightly. 8. When the cooking is complete, refrigerate the apples while you prepare the piecrust. 9. Cut each piecrust into 2 (10 cm) circles. You should have 8 circles of crust. 10. Lay the piecrusts on a work surface. Divide the apple filling among the piecrusts, mounding the mixture in the centre of each round. 11. Fold each piecrust over so the top layer of crust is about 2 cm short of the bottom layer. (The edges should not meet.) Use the back of a fork to seal the edges. 12. Insert the crisper plate into the air fryer basket, and preheat the air fryer at 205 °C for 3 minutes. 13. Once the unit is preheated, spray the crisper plate with cooking oil, line the air fryer basket with parchment paper, and spray it with cooking oil. Working in batches, place the hand pies into the air fryer basket in a layer. 14. Air Fry the pies at 205 °C for 10 minutes. 15. When the cooking is complete, let the hand pies cool for 5 minutes before removing from the air fryer basket. 16. Do the same with the remaining pies. 17. Serve and enjoy.
Per Serving: Calories 570; Fat 29.25g; Sodium 469mg; Carbs 74.49g; Fibre 3.4g; Sugar 13.51g; Protein 3.57g

Great Funnel Cake

Prep Time: 10 minutes | Cook Time: 5 minutes | Serves: 4

Oil, for spraying
125 g self-rising flour, plus more for dusting
245 g fat-free vanilla Greek yogurt
½ teaspoon ground cinnamon
30 g confectioners' sugar

1. Turn on the air fryer and preheat it to 190 °C. Line the air fryer basket with parchment and sprinkle with oil. 2. Mix together the flour, yogurt, and cinnamon in a bowl until the mixture forms a ball. 3. Place the dough on a lightly floured work surface and knead for about 2 minutes. 4. Cut the dough into 4 equal pieces, then cut each of those into 6 pieces. 5.Roll the pieces into 20 – 25 cmlong ropes. Loosely mound the ropes into 4 piles of 6 ropes. 6.Place the dough piles in the air fryer basket and spray liberally with oil. 7.Cook for 5 minutes. 8.Dust with the icing' sugar before serving.
Per Serving: Calories 148; Fat 1.44g; Sodium 377 mg; Carbs 30.12g; Fibre 1g; Sugar 6.58g; Protein 3.27 g

Irresistible Churro Bites

Prep Time: 5 minutes | Cook Time: 6 minutes | Serves: 12

Oil, for spraying
1 (430 g) package frozen puffed pastry, thawed
200 g granulated sugar
1 tablespoon ground cinnamon
60 g icing sugar
1 tablespoon milk

1. Turn on the air fryer and preheat it to 205 °C. Line the air fryer basket with parchment and sprinkle with oil. 2.Unfold the puff pastry onto a clean work surface. Using a sharp knife, cut the dough into 36 bite-size pieces. 3. Place the dough pieces in one layer in the air fryer basket, taking care not to let the pieces touch or overlap. 4. Cook for 3 minutes, flip, and cook for 3 more minutes. 5. Mix together the granulated sugar and cinnamon in a bowl. 6. Whisk together the icing sugar and milk in a bowl. 7.Dredge the bites in the cinnamon-sugar mixture until evenly coated. 8. Serve with the icing on the side for dipping.
Per Serving: Calories 279; Fat 15.8g; Sodium 104mg; Carbs 31.7g; Fibre 1g; Sugar 12.61g; Protein 3.08g

Irresistible Cherry Pie

Prep Time: 15 minutes | **Cook Time:** 35 minutes | **Serves:** 6

Plain flour, for dusting
2 refrigerated piecrusts, at room temperature
1 (310 g) can cherry pie filling
1 egg
1 tablespoon water
1 tablespoon sugar

1. Dust a work surface with flour and place the piecrust on it. Roll out the piecrust. Invert a shallow air fryer baking pan, or your own pie pan that fits inside the air fryer basket, on top of the dough. Trim the dough around the pan, making your cut 1 cm wider than the pan itself. 2. Repeat with the second piecrust but make the cut the same size as or slightly smaller than the pan. 3. Put the larger crust in the bottom of the baking pan. Don't stretch the dough. Gently press it into the pan. 4. Spoon in enough cherry pie filling to fill the crust. Do not overfill. 5. Using a knife or pizza cutter, cut the second piecrust into 2.5 cm wide strips. Weave the strips in a lattice pattern over the top of the cherry pie filling. 6. Insert the crisper plate into the air fryer basket and the air fryer basket into the unit. Preheat the air fryer at 160 °C for 3 minutes on Bake mode. 7. Whisk the egg and water in a small bowl. Gently brush the egg wash over the top of the pie. Sprinkle with the sugar and cover the pie with aluminum foil. 8. Once the unit is preheated, place the pie into the air fryer basket. 9. Bake the pie at 160 °C for 35 minutes. 10. After 30 minutes, remove the foil and resume cooking for 3 to 5 minutes more. The finished pie should have a flaky golden brown crust and bubbling pie filling. 11. When the cooking is complete, serve warm. Refrigerate leftovers for a few days.
Per Serving: Calories 351; Fat 16.95g; Sodium 410mg; Carbs 44.8g; Fibre 1.3g; Sugar 1.33g; Protein 4.71g

Wonderful Strawberry-Rhubarb Crumble

Prep Time: 10 minutes | **Cook Time:** 15 minutes | **Serves:** 6

230 g sliced fresh strawberries
90 g sliced rhubarb
55 g granulated sugar
70 g quick-cooking oatmeal
60 g whole-wheat pastry flour, or plain flour
55 g packed light brown sugar
½ teaspoon ground cinnamon
3 tablespoons unsalted butter, melted

1. Insert the crisper plate into the air fryer basket, and preheat the air fryer at 190 °C for 3 minutes on Bake mode. 2. In a suitable round metal baking pan, combine the strawberries, rhubarb, and granulated sugar. 3. Stir the oatmeal, flour, brown sugar, and cinnamon in a bowl, then stir in the melted butter until crumbly. 4. Sprinkle the crumble mixture over the fruit. 5. Once the unit is preheated, place the pan into the air fryer basket. 6. Bake the food for 17 minutes. 7. After about 12 minutes, check the crumble. If the fruit is bubbling and the topping is golden brown, it is done. If not, resume cooking. 8. When the cooking is complete, serve warm.
Per Serving: Calories 170; Fat 5.19g; Sodium 47mg; Carbs 29.59g; Fibre 2.9g; Sugar 17.28g; Protein3.39g

Delicious Berry Cheese Cake

Prep Time: 5 minutes | Cook Time: 10 minutes | **Serves:** 4

Oil, for spraying
200 g cream cheese
6 tablespoons sugar
1 tablespoon sour cream
1 large egg
½ teaspoon vanilla extract
¼ teaspoon lemon juice
70 g fresh mixed berries

1.Turn on the air fryer and preheat it to 175 °C. Line the air fryer basket with parchment and sprinkle with oil. 2. Add the cream cheese, sugar, sour cream, egg, vanilla, and lemon juice to a blender, and blend them until smooth. Pour the mixture into a 10 cm spring form pan. 3. Place the pan in the air fryer basket. 4. Cook the mixture for 8 to 10 minutes. 5.Refrigerate the cheesecake in the pan for at least 2 hours. 6.Release the sides from the spring form pan, top the cheesecake with the mixed berries,.
Per Serving: Calories 306; Fat 20.36g; Sodium 307mg; Carbs 26.08g; Fibre 0.5g; Sugar 20.25g; Protein 5.56g

Wonderful Big Chocolate Cookie

Prep Time: 7 minutes | **Cook Time:** 9 minutes | **Serves:** 4

3 tablespoons butter, at room temperature
70 g plus 1 tablespoon light brown sugar
1 egg yolk
60 g plain flour
2 tablespoons ground white chocolate
¼ teaspoon baking soda
½ teaspoon vanilla extract
125 g semisweet chocolate chips
Nonstick flour-infused baking spray

1. Beat together the butter and brown sugar until fluffy in a bowl. Stir in the egg yolk. 2. Add the flour, white chocolate, baking soda, and vanilla and mix well. Stir in the chocolate chips. 3. Line a 15-by-5-cm round baking pan with parchment paper. Spray the parchment paper with flour-infused baking spray. 4. Insert the crisper plate into the air fryer basket, and preheat the air fryer at 150 °C for 3 minutes on Bake mode. 5. Spread the batter into the prepared pan, leaving a 1 cm border on all sides. 6. Once the unit is preheated, place the pan into the air fryer basket. 7. Bake the batter for 9 minutes. 8. When the cooking is complete, the cookie should be light brown and just barely set. Remove the pan from the air fryer basket and let cool for 10 minutes. 9. Remove the cookie from the pan, remove the parchment paper, and let cool completely on a wire rack.
Per Serving: Calories 337; Fat 14.67g; Sodium 161mg; Carbs 48.16g; Fibre 0.4g; Sugar 21.87g; Protein 4.05 g

Easy S'more

Prep Time: 5 minutes | **Cook Time:** 30 seconds | **Serves:** 4.

Oil, for spraying
8 digestive biscuits
2 (40 g) chocolate bars
4 large marshmallows

1.Line the air fryer basket with parchment and sprinkle with oil. 2.Place 4 graham cracker squares in the air fryer basket. 3. Break the chocolate bars in half and place 1 piece on top of each disgestive biscuit. Top with 1 marshmallow. 4. Cook them at 185 °C for 30 seconds. 5.Top with the remaining digestive biscuit, and enjoy.
Per Serving: Calories 247; Fat 13.64g; Sodium 78mg; Carbs 28.49g; Fibre 3.4g; Sugar 13.69g; Protein 3.14g

Perfect Beignets

Prep Time: 15 minutes | **Cook Time:** 6 minutes | **Serves:** 9

Oil, for greasing and spraying
375 g plain flour, plus more for dusting
1½ teaspoons salt
1 (2¼-teaspoon) envelope active dry yeast
240 ml milk
2 tablespoons packed light brown sugar
1 tablespoon unsalted butter
1 large egg
120 g icing sugar

1. Sprinkle some oil in a big bowl. 2. Mix together the flour, salt, and yeast in a small bowl. 3. Pour the milk into a glass measuring cup and microwave in 1-minute intervals until it boils. 4. Mix together the brown sugar and butter. Pour in the hot milk in a bowl and whisk until the sugar has dissolved. Let cool to room temperature. 5. Whisk the egg into the cooled milk mixture and fold in the flour mixture until a dough forms. 6. On a lightly floured work surface, knead the dough for 3 to 5 minutes. 7. Place the dough in the oiled bowl and cover with a clean kitchen towel. Let rise in a warm place for about 1 hour. 8. Roll the dough out on a lightly floured work surface until it's about ½ cm thick. Cut the dough into 7.5 cm squares and place them on a lightly floured baking sheet. Cover loosely with a kitchen towel and let rise for about 30 minutes until doubled in size. 9. Line the air fryer basket with parchment and sprinkle with oil. 10. Place the dough squares in the air fryer basket and sprinkle with oil. 11. Cook at 200 °C for 3 minutes, flip, spray with oil, and cook for 3 more minutes. 12. Dust with the icing sugar before serving.
Per Serving: Calories 419; Fat 3.23g; Sodium 416 mg; Carbs 92.61g; Fibre 1.4g; Sugar 59.79g; Protein 5.97 g

Quick and Easy Apple Pie Egg Rolls

Prep Time: 10 **minutes** | **Cook Time:** 8 minutes | **Serves:** 6

Oil, for spraying
1 (525 g) can apple pie filling
1 tablespoon plain flour
½ teaspoon lemon juice
¼ teaspoon ground nutmeg
¼ teaspoon ground cinnamon
6 egg roll wrappers

1.Turn on the air fryer and preheat it to 205 °C. Line the air fryer basket with parchment and sprinkle with oil. 2. Mix together the pie filling, flour, lemon juice, nutmeg, and cinnamon in a bowl. 3. Lay out the egg roll wrappers on a work surface and spoon a dollop of pie filling in the centre of each. 4.Fill a small bowl with water. Dip your finger in the water and, working one at a time, moisten the edges of the wrappers. Fold the wrapper like an envelope: First fold one corner into the centre. Fold each side corner in, and then fold over the remaining corner, making sure each corner overlaps a bit and the moistened edges stay closed. Use additional water and your fingers to seal any open edges. 5.Place the rolls in the air fryer basket and spray liberally with oil.   6.Cook for 4 minutes, flip, spray with oil, and cook for 4 more minutes.
Per Serving: Calories 198; Fat 0.63g; Sodium 230 mg; Carbs 45.59g; Fibre 1.7g; Sugar 13.71g; Protein 3.38g

Simple Blueberry Hand Pies

Prep Time: 15 minutes | **Cook Time:** 10 minutes | **Serves:** 12

Oil, for spraying
250 g plain flour
¼ teaspoon baking soda
¼ teaspoon salt
120 ml vegetable oil
80 ml buttermilk
1 (525 g) can blueberry pie filling
1 large egg, beaten
120 g icing sugar
2 tablespoons milk

1. Line the air fryer basket with parchment and sprinkle with oil. 2. Mix together the flour, baking soda, and salt in a bowl. Add the vegetable oil and buttermilk and mix together until the mixture forms a ball. 3. Roll out the dough on a work surface until it is about ½ cm thick. Using a 10 cm biscuit cutter, cut the dough into 12 circles. 4. Spoon a dollop of pie filling in the centre of each dough circle. 5. Fill a small bowl with water. Wet the edges of the dough with water, then fold the dough in half and press the edges with a fork to seal it closed. 6. Brush the pies with the egg. Using a fork, poke small holes in the top of each pie. 7. Place the pies in the air fryer basket, taking care not to overlap, and sprinkle oil over them. 8. Cook the pies at 175 °C for 10 minutes. Let cool completely. 9. Whisk together the icing sugar and milk and set aside in a bowl. 10. Have a piece of parchment paper or a large plate nearby. Dip the pies in the glaze mixture, turning to coat both sides. 11. Use a fork to lift them out of the bowl and to help shake off any excess. Place them on the parchment and let the glaze dry before serving.
Per Serving: Calories 245; Fat 9.85g; Sodium 114mg; Carbs37.66g; Fibre 11g; Sugar 15.51g; Protein 2.73g

Luscious "Grilled" Watermelon

Prep Time: 10 minutes | **Cook Time:** 4 minutes | **Serves:** 4

2 teaspoons olive oil
2 tablespoons fresh orange juice
1 teaspoon orange zest
1 tablespoon granular sweetener
⅛ teaspoon salt
450 g 2.5 cm watermelon cubes
1 tablespoon chopped fresh mint

1. Preheat the air fryer at 190 °C for 3 minutes. 2. Whisk together olive oil, orange juice, orange zest, sweetener, and salt in a bowl. Toss in watermelon cubes and let marinate 10 minutes. 3. Add watermelon mixture to the air fryer basket, and then cook for 4 minutes, tossing halfway through. 4. Serve warm or at room temperature, garnished with fresh mint.
Per Serving: Calories 73; Fat 2.5g; Sodium 79mg; Carbs 13.32g; Fibre 0.7g; Sugar 10.92g; Protein 1.02g

Perfect Grilled Peaches

Prep Time: 5 **minutes** | **Cook Time:** 10 minutes | **Serves:** 4

Oil, for spraying
15 g digestive biscuit cracker crumbs
55 g light brown sugar
8 tablespoons unsalted butter, cubed
¼ teaspoon cinnamon
2 peaches, pitted and cut into quarters
4 scoops vanilla ice cream

1.Line the air fryer basket with parchment and sprinkle with oil. 2. Mix together the digestive biscuit crumbs, brown sugar, butter, and cinnamon with a fork until crumbly in a bowl. 3. Place the peach wedges in the air fryer basket, skin-side up. 4. Cook at 175 °C for 5 minutes, flip, and sprinkle with a spoonful of the graham cracker mixture. Cook for 5 more minutes. 5.Top with a scoop of vanilla ice cream and any remaining crumble mixture. Serve immediately.
Per Serving: Calories 472; Fat 31.54g; Sodium 127mg; Carbs 42.91g; Fibre 1.7g; Sugar 37.84g; Protein 6.01g

Delicious Meringue Cookies

Prep Time: 15 minutes | **Cook Time:** 90 minutes | **Serves:** 10

Oil, for spraying
4 large egg whites
190 g sugar
Pinch cream of tartar

1. Turn on the air fryer and preheat it to 60 °C. Line the air fryer basket with parchment and sprinkle with oil. 2. Whisk together the egg whites and sugar in a bowl. Fill a small saucepan halfway with water, place it over medium heat, and bring to a light simmer. Place the bowl with the egg whites on the saucepan, making sure the bottom of the bowl does not touch the water. Whisk the mixture until the sugar is dissolved. 3. Transfer the mixture to a large bowl and add the cream of tartar. Using an electric mixer, beat the mixture on high until it is glossy and stiff peaks form. Transfer the mixture to a piping bag or a zip-top plastic bag with a corner cut off. 4. Pipe rounds into the air fryer basket. 5. Cook for 1 hour 30 minutes. 6. Turn off the air fryer and let the meringues cool completely inside. The residual heat will continue to dry them out.
Per Serving: Calories 47; Fat 0.02g; Sodium 22mg; Carbs 10.26g; Fibre 0g; Sugar 9.87g; Protein 1.44g

Unbeatable Gooey Lemon Bars

Prep Time: 15 minutes | **Cook Time:** 25 minutes | **Serves:** 6

95 g whole-wheat pastry flour
2 tablespoons icing sugar
55 g butter, melted
95 g granulated sugar
1 tablespoon packed grated lemon zest
60 ml freshly squeezed lemon juice
⅛ teaspoon sea salt
60 g unsweetened plain applesauce
2 teaspoons cornflour
¾ teaspoon baking powder
Cooking oil spray (sunflower, safflower, or refined coconut)

1. Stir the flour, icing sugar, and melted butter just until well combined in a bowl. Place in the refrigerator. 2. Stir the granulated sugar, lemon zest and juice, salt, applesauce, cornflour, and baking powder in a bowl. 3. Insert the crisper plate into the air fryer basket, and preheat the air fryer at 175 °C for 3 minutes on Bake mode. 4. Spray a 15-by-5-cm round pan lightly with cooking oil. Remove the crust mixture from the refrigerator and gently press it into the bottom of the prepared pan in an even layer. 5. Once the unit is preheated, place the pan into the air fryer basket. 6. Bake the dish at 175 °C for 25 minutes. 7. After 5 minutes, check the crust. It should be slightly firm to the touch. Remove the pan and spread the lemon filling over the crust. Reinsert the pan into the air fryer basket and resume baking for 18 to 20 minutes. 8. When baking is complete, let cool for 30 minutes. Refrigerate to cool completely. Cut into pieces.
Per Serving: Calories 173; Fat 8.14g; Sodium 114 mg; Carbs 24.91g; Fibre 1.8; Sugar 12.1g; Protein 2.13 g

This article will dispel all of your questions regarding the healthiness of air frying and the use of air fryers.

Overall, it's a fairly nice piece of technology. It may satisfy all of your cravings for mouth-watering, delectable fried cuisine without using any oil. The results are far superior to oil frying, and your kitchen is also kept clean. The air fryer excels in emulating deep frying, even if it performs a commendable job of cooking various types of meat and vegetables.

This article will explain the advantages of using an air fryer for cooking as well as the drawbacks. It will also provide you with a list of mouth-watering dishes that you can prepare in the comfort of your own home. Additionally, it will explain how air fryers operate and their numerous applications for them.

Appendix 1 Measurement Conversion Chart

VOLUME EQUIVALENTS (LIQUID)

US STANDARD	US STANDARD (OUNCES)	METRIC (APPROXIMATE)
2 tablespoons	1 fl.oz	30 mL
¼ cup	2 fl.oz	60 mL
½ cup	4 fl.oz	120 mL
1 cup	8 fl.oz	240 mL
1½ cup	12 fl.oz	355 mL
2 cups or 1 pint	16 fl.oz	475 mL
4 cups or 1 quart	32 fl.oz	1 L
1 gallon	128 fl.oz	4 L

VOLUME EQUIVALENTS (DRY)

US STANDARD	METRIC (APPROXIMATE)
⅛ teaspoon	0.5 mL
¼ teaspoon	1 mL
½ teaspoon	2 mL
¾ teaspoon	4 mL
1 teaspoon	5 mL
1 tablespoon	15 mL
¼ cup	59 mL
½ cup	118 mL
¾ cup	177 mL
1 cup	235 mL
2 cups	475 mL
3 cups	700 mL
4 cups	1 L

TEMPERATURES EQUIVALENTS

FAHRENHEIT(F)	CELSIUS（C）(APPROXIMATE)
225 °F	107 °C
250 °F	120 °C
275 °F	135 °C
300 °F	150 °C
325 °F	160 °C
350 °F	180 °C
375 °F	190 °C
400 °F	205 °C
425 °F	220 °C
450 °F	235 °C
475 °F	245 °C
500 °F	260 °C

WEIGHT EQUIVALENTS

US STANDARD	METRIC (APPROXINATE)
1 ounce	28 g
2 ounces	57 g
5 ounces	142 g
10 ounces	284 g
15 ounces	425 g
16 ounces (1 pound)	455 g
1.5pounds	680 g
2pounds	907 g

Appendix 2 Air Fryer Cooking Chart

vegetables	Temp (℉)	Time (min)	Meat	Temp (℉)	Time (min)
Asparagus (1-inch slices)	400	5	Bacon	400	5 to 7
Beets (sliced)	350	25	Beef Eye Round Roast (4 lbs.)	390	50 to 60
Beets (whole)	400	40	Burger (4 oz.)	370	16 to 20
Bell Peppers (sliced)	350	13	Chicken Breasts, bone-in (1.25 lbs.)	370	25
Broccoli	400	6	Chicken Breasts, boneless (4 oz.)	380	12
Brussels Sprouts (halved)	380	15	Chicken Drumsticks (2.5 lbs.)	370	20
Carrots(½-inch slices)	380	15	Chicken Thighs, bone-in (2 lbs.)	380	22
Cauliflower (florets)	400	12	Chicken Thighs, boneless (1.5 lbs.)	380	18 to 20
Eggplant (1½-inch cubes)	400	15	Chicken Legs, bone-in (1.75 lbs.)	380	30
Fennel (quartered)	370	15	Chicken Wings (2 lbs.)	400	12
Mushrooms (¼-inch slices)	400	5	Flank Steak (1.5 lbs.)	400	12
Onion (pearl)	400	10	Game Hen (halved, 2 lbs.)	390	20
Parsnips (½-inch chunks)	380	5	Loin (2 lbs.)	360	55
Peppers (1-inch chunks)	400	15	London Broil (2 lbs.)	400	20 to 28
Potatoes (baked, whole)	400	40	Meatballs (3-inch)	380	10
Squash (½-inch chunks)	400	12	Rack of Lamb (1.5-2 lbs.)	380	22
Tomatoes (cherry)	400	4	Sausages	380	15
Zucchni (½-inch sticks)	400	12	Whole Chicken (6.5 lbs.)	360	75

Fish and Seafood			Frozen Foods		
Calamari (8 oz.)	400	4	Onion Rings (12 oz.)	400	8
Fish Fillet (1-inch, 8 oz.)	400	10	Thin French Fries (20 oz.)	400	14
Salmon Fillet (6 oz.)	380	12	Thick French Fries (17 oz.)	400	18
Tuna Steak	400	7 to 10	Pot Sticks (10 oz.)	400	8
Scallops	400	5 to 7	Fish Sticks (10 oz.)	400	10
Shrimp	400	5	Fish Fillets (½-inch, 10 oz.)	400	14

Appendix 3 Recipes Index